Naoyuki and Ruth Taned

Education for Absolute Pitch

A new way to learn piano

Handbook for teachers and parents
for the **We Hear and Play** system

translated by Christopher Aruffo

Acoustic Learning, Inc.
Gainesville, Florida

Licensed from Schott

www.wehearandplay.com
www.acousticlearning.com

The *We Hear and Play* System

The complete *We Hear and Play* instructional system
consists of the following materials:

- Education for Absolute Pitch: A New Way to Learn Piano
- *We Hear and Play*, Volume 1
- *We Hear and Play*, Volume 2
- *We Hear and Play*, Volume 3
- Colored balls (set of 7) in *We Hear and Play* colors
- Colored stickers (set of 7) in *We Hear and Play* colors

These materials are available for purchase at www.wehearandplay.com.

ISBN 0-9761435-1-8
Photos by Photo Design Studio Mihaly, Karlsruhe, Germany (except Figs. 10-11)
Illustration by Andreas Schürmann
©2005 Acoustic Learning, Inc.
Title of the original German edition: Erziehung zum absoluten Gehör.
©1993 Schott Musik International GmbH & Co. KG, Mainz, Germany.
This translation is published and sold by permission of Schott, the owner of all
rights to publish and sell the same.

SECOND PRINTING

About This Book

Ruth and Nayouki Taneda have taught music to children for more than 30 years. In this handbook, they show how it is possible to develop absolute pitch (also known as "perfect pitch") in small children, giving them a skill previously thought of as an innate privilege of only especially gifted musicians. The authors discuss the myths related to absolute pitch, and they describe the effects of absolute pitch on a child's musical upbringing. In the process, they present a new style of instrumental instruction.

For teachers and parents— whose cooperation is essential during a child's earliest stages— this handbook is a companion to the three-volume *We Hear and Play*, a piano curriculum for children starting from between ages 3 and 4½ years old. The most important goals of *We Hear and Play* are

- Acquisition of absolute pitch

- Development of rhythmic feeling

- Introduction to piano playing, with emphasis on "good sound"

Additional teaching goals for *We Hear and Play* include

- Full interactivity with music

- Improved playing technique

- Capacity for musical expression

- Creative interplay with the piano through improvisation

- Introduction to harmony

- Ability to read and write musical notes

- Increased ability to concentrate

How to Use This Book

For the Teacher

This book is designed to be a practical guide. You can start right away by

- Reviewing the materials you'll need (page 4)
- Familiarizing yourself with the method's four games (page 8)
- Studying the suggested first lesson (page 22)

When playing the games, it's essential to ignore the child's mistakes, and to praise their efforts as well as their successes. The authors discuss the psychological support for this approach on page 31 and in other places in the book.

As you approach the piano, you will want to familiarize yourself with the principles of piano technique in small children (page 24), the theory and application of using colored notes (page 59), and the philosophy of training preschool children (page 31). Step-by-step guidance for the *We Hear and Play* piano books begins on page 34.

To learn more about the Taneda method, its goals and philosophy, read the Preface and Foreword on page 1.

To learn more about absolute pitch, turn to page 76.

For answers to frequently asked questions, turn to page 78.

Advanced training concepts start on page 58.

For the Parents

This ear-training method consists of games you will play with your child. You play the games at home, and as you play, your child will learn absolute pitch.

Piano playing is introduced in conjunction with these games. Although this handbook is written for a music teacher, who will guide you in how to practice piano with your child, you can cooperate at home while having only a minimal knowledge of music and musical notation. You do need to know what a *chord* and an *octave* are, and you need to know how to play a piano chord. Your instructor will be sure to show these to you. Even if you can't read music, you will be able to match the note colors along with your child.

When playing the games, it's essential to ignore your child's mistakes and praise their successes. The authors discuss the psychological support for this approach on page 31 and in other places in the book.

To begin playing the training games, turn to page 8. Your child's music teacher will guide you when it is time for your child to begin playing the piano.

To play the training games, you will need

- A well-tuned piano in good condition
- A stool for your child's feet
- One or more sets of seven small balls in red, blue, yellow, orange, purple, grey, and green
- Colored self-adhesive dots (³/₄ inch) in these same seven colors
- *We Hear and Play*, Volume One

To learn more about the Taneda method, its goals and philosophy, read the Preface and Foreword on page 1.

To learn more about absolute pitch, turn to page 76.

For answers to frequently asked questions, turn to page 78.

Table of Contents

Before you Begin

Preface

I feel highly privileged to present you with this groundbreaking work from Ruth and Naoyuki Taneda. I first encountered this book, in its original German, while conducting research on absolute pitch and how to teach it to adults. I began translating the book out of curiosity, and I finished due to utter fascination. The Taneda method is what every parent has been hoping for.

The goal of the Taneda method is total musical literacy. The method teaches *absolute pitch* (also known as "perfect pitch") which is the foundation for a natural, instinctive relationship to musical language. Think about how clearly you hear your own language: when you hear words, you can write down every letter; when you speak, you compose sentences instantly and effortlessly. A Taneda student enjoys this same deep understanding of music. The student will gain the power to express musical ideas with freedom and joy. The Taneda method allows a child to "think in music" as a language all its own.

This book tells you not to ignore the ear-training exercises in favor of piano playing. This is because piano playing is ultimately a direct extension of the listening exercises. The piano becomes a kind of "typewriter" with which a child speaks their new musical language. They must hear the sounds mentally to play the instrument fluently and effortlessly. The Taneda ear training techniques are the foundation of their piano instruction method.

The time has come for the Taneda method to be revealed to the world. I find it easy to believe that any parent would gladly teach their child to know pitch sounds as surely as they know colors. Who knows how the world may be changed by this strange new language? The coming generation will discover a meaning and delight in sound which has, until now, been inaccessible to humankind.

- Christopher Aruffo

Foreword

Music literature, when discussing piano methods or music psychology, sometimes refers to *absolute pitch*, also known as "perfect pitch." Absolute pitch is the ability to recognize a specific musical pitch without a reference tone. Many authors believe that absolute pitch is an innate, genetic capacity which can't be learned. Our extensive experience contradicts this. We shall show that absolute pitch is a skill that can be learned.

This handbook doesn't intend to exaggerate the significance of absolute pitch. We wish to explore the possibilities that it offers for musical training, and to observe the phenomenon studiously.

For a healthy, normal child, absolute-pitch instruction should begin no later than age 4½. Ideally, a child will start at age 3. If a child begins to develop their ear at this age, following our methods, after only one year they will acquire the basis for absolute pitch. They will possess absolute pitch after approximately two years. If they continue to study music, their ear continues to develop even further. Adults typically don't expect that a child can learn absolute pitch, so they neglect this most favorable stage of development. If instruction begins after a child is 4½ years old, success is not guaranteed.

Our curriculum also teaches the child to play the piano while they are learning absolute pitch. The piano is the best instrument for absolute-pitch education. The child's family should own a relatively new piano that they keep precisely tuned and in good condition, or absolute pitch training is impossible. For the lessons, parents should use our three-volume publication *We Hear and Play*, which we developed through extensive work with children. This work made clear how children may be taught absolute pitch, as a basis for early musical training. On completing our course, a child may continue to develop their piano skills or may change to any other instrument.

In *We Hear and Play* sounds are associated with colors. Therefore, the child being trained must be able to distinguish and name colors. A child between 3 and 3½ years old can normally do this.

Our instructional method is designed for tutoring a single child, because each child in a group is likely to be at a different stage of development. This makes it impossible to be sure of providing everything they need.

The instructional atmosphere must be positive. This is critical. Children can only be trained if the process is enjoyable and fun. Only then will they be ready to cooperate. Mechanical drilling or forced instruction can quickly teach children to dislike the training and resist achievement.

For this method to succeed, the teacher's personality is decisive. The teacher must be loving, patient, and inventive; above all, they must respect the childlike personality. This handbook describes our teaching objectives in detail and provides practical advice. Within this pedagogic structure, every teacher must identify the essential training points and find appropriate ways to present the material to each child.

Teaching preschool children calls for a large commitment. Despite the simple appearance of the instructional material, the task is demanding and requires an intensive relationship. The teacher must be aware of their responsibility for the child's developing personality. Based on this awareness, the use of this method enriches children, parents, and teachers alike.

Will the children who are given this training become the musical elite of the future? Not necessarily. This material is not intended to make all students into musicians. We created this process to enrich any child's lifelong understanding of the world of music.

We want to thank the Ettlingen Music School and the Mainz Academy for Music Pedagogics, who promoted this instructional work, as well as all the piano educators who have reported to us their experiences of training children with this method. With much gratitude, we remember Mr. Lothar Friedrich, the Schott publishing house lecturer who supported *We Hear and Play* even from its origin phase. He passed away all too soon.

- Naoyuki and Ruth Taneda

Materials You Will Need

Piano

A teacher must have a well-tuned piano in their instruction room. It should be tuned to $A = 442.5$ Hz, which should match the tuning of the student's piano.

At home, the child must have a well-tuned piano in good condition. The piano tones should sound neither harsh nor muted. The keys should be neither too easy nor too hard to press down. The instrument should be tuned, and mechanically checked, at least semiannually. There should be a stable, height-adjustable chair (or stool) in front of the piano.

Footstool

Children also require a footstool (Figure 1). It should be high enough so that the child's feet can rest comfortably, with the thighs almost horizontal. As a child proceeds through the years of instruction, the footstool should be adapted to the body's growth; it is usually necessary until age eight or nine. Specialty piano stores sell adjustable footstools for children. It is also possible to have a footstool for each individual child and to shorten its legs at appropriate times during the child's growth. This can help pedagogically, since shortening the stool becomes a significant experience for the child, showing them that they have grown.

Figure 1

Figure 2

The Norwegian firm Stokke sells a child's piano chair called "Kinderzeat," which integrates seat and foot support (Figure 2). As a piano chair it has several advantages: first, it is stable and non-tilting; second, it doesn't slip on non-carpeted floors; third, parents can firmly adjust its height so that the child cannot change it; fourth, the child can lean back and relax into the back of the seat.

Colored Dots

In *We Hear and Play*, colors are assigned to the sounds of the white keys:

C	D	E	F	G	A	B
red	yellow	green	orange	blue	grey	purple

Prior to starting instruction, a child should already be able to recognize these colors.

To mark the piano keys, teacher and parents both need a sufficient supply of self-adhesive colored dots. These may often be purchased from an office-supply store, but are not always available in the necessary colors. Dots of all seven colors are available from the *We Hear and Play* website (www.wehearandplay.com). These dots must be applied to the keyboard before the lessons begin, one centimeter from the front edge of the key. At the beginning level, only the area from low F through middle G should be marked. When expanding the playing area to new octaves, every key in each new octave should be marked. At the final level, all keys are marked.

To remove the colored dots, the best solution is a petroleum cleaner which does not damage the keys. One such product is sold under the brand name "Goo Gone." The glue residue can be removed by moistening a soft cloth with the cleaner and rubbing it over the keys. The chemical should, of course, be stored in a place inaccessible to children.

Sometimes children want to play songs not included in *We Hear and Play*. For these songs, the teacher should use note sheets with two or four large staves, which can be found in music shops. Using felt-tip pens or colored pencils, the teacher should write down the desired songs using colored notes of the same size as in *We Hear and Play*.

At the beginning of *We Hear and Play* instruction, a child learns to assign each finger to a certain color and key. Colored nail polish is often popular, to mark the colors on each finger. Nail polish has the additional advantage of staying on the fingernails for some time.

Colored Balls

The primary ear training game requires a set of colored balls in the seven note colors. These balls are the critical component of the ear training games. The teacher should have an ample supply of balls in the instruction room. Parents should also have at least one set to play with at home. Sets of these balls are available at the *We Hear and Play* website (www.wehearandplay.com).

An alternative to balls is homemade beanbags, filled with small beans, rice, or cotton. The balls or beanbags must clearly and recognizably correspond to the colors used in *We Hear and Play*. Any objects used for the ear training games should be relatively featureless, and of solid color; it is not recommended to use toys with many parts, or to use objects which have multiple layers of color, even if they are different shades of the same color.

Note references

In this handbook, notes will usually be referred to with their octave designations, such as "high C," "low F," "middle G," et cetera. These terms refer to the following areas of the keyboard:

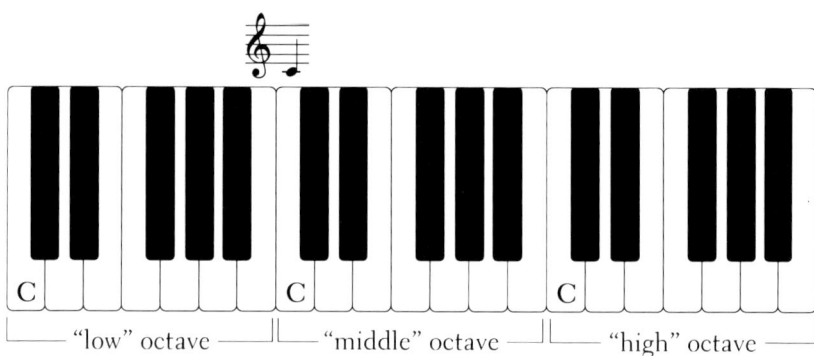

Personal Preparation

For a 3-4½ year old child, each instruction period is usually about 30 minutes. This does not mean that the child practices piano or rhythm for half an hour without interruption. The younger the child, the shorter the active training phases should be, interrupted by recovery and game phases. As the child's age increases, the instruction time will be more fully used. When the child has reached Volume Three of *We Hear and Play*, it may become necessary to incrementally raise the lesson time to 45 minutes.

Parents who want to raise their child using the *We Hear and Play* curriculum should have a healthy attitude toward their child's musical achievement. This does not mean a pathological ambition, which strives only for maximum performance. It means avoiding indifference. The parents should be able to express a loving attitude toward the child and develop a suitable practice system with them.

Because the teacher must maintain a strong relationship with the child, parents must resist seeing the teacher as a rival. If difficulties appear in the child's instruction, the parents should be very patient; they should never frivolously interrupt the musical training once it has begun. The value of a positive attitude toward the process cannot be overestimated.

As with all training processes, there should not be frequent and lengthy interruptions in musical education, whether through frequent long vacations or lack of discipline. The parents should allow a routine to include *We Hear and Play* instruction in every weekend or vacation. The instruction is not useful if it is not reinforced at home; without regular instruction and practice, it is impossible to develop absolute pitch. With persistent interruptions, a child may backslide and lose their musical ability entirely.

Joy and success can occur if musical training is integrated into daily life like meals, sleep, games, or brushing teeth. Then the musical work becomes an essential and stimulating part of the child's routine— and this is the best defense against boredom or undesirable exposure to television.

Basic Method
Absolute Pitch Training

The hearing exercises are divided into two types: *chord sounds* and *single sounds*, each of which has its corresponding game.

Game One: Peekaboo

Absolute pitch develops primarily from recognizing chords. If a child learns to recognize two chords absolutely, they can gradually hear single pitches absolutely. Therefore, the I, II, and III chords (Volume One, page 5) are an indispensable element of the listening instruction. The child learns these chords by associating their sounds with three stuffed animals they have selected. Each of the animals is assigned to a chord, and the assignments are permanent.

Chord I is introduced in the first lesson. The child should select and bring one stuffed animal to the session. Stuffed animals are best because they can talk, act, and converse, unlike inanimate objects such as cars and trains, which are not recommended. A doll can be used instead of a stuffed animal, but two different stuffed animals should be selected for the other two chords. This is because the toys often have no names but are called what they are: "doll," "bear," "rabbit," etc. If each of the three chords are assigned to different toys all called "doll," this creates problems in distinguishing the toys and therefore the chord sounds.

The first stuffed animal is also important for introducing the teacher to the child. A child is often shy when meeting a new person and will sometimes reject the new person altogether. The more a grown-up pressures a child to make contact, the more the child may hide and resist. But if the teacher begins conversing with the stuffed animal, they will draw the child out. The teacher can, for example, ask a stuffed animal about its favorite activities, games, or foods. The child will become curious and willingly slip into the role of the animal to answer the questions. This is a good way for a teacher to learn about a child without direct confrontation.

Once the child has accepted the teacher, the teacher can introduce the "peekaboo game." The teacher tells the child that they have a pretty sound for the animal, a sound it will surely like. The teacher then plays Chord I:

Chord I must be played exclusively in this octave. At no time should it be played in a higher or lower octave. All notes must be struck simultaneously, at an average volume.

Once the animal hears this sound, it is "happy" and comes to the piano. Subsequently, the teacher plays a random cluster of higher or lower notes, and explains to the child that the animal wants to hide itself now. But, at the reappearance of Chord I, the animal comes out of its hiding place and to the piano (Figure 3). The teacher should demonstrate this action for the child to imitate.

If the child understands the game's rule, the teacher continues to play Chord I, alternated with high or low clusters. The teacher should never play major or minor chords alternated with Chord I but should use more dissonant sounds. Gradually, through attentive listening, the child will associate the animal with the chord.

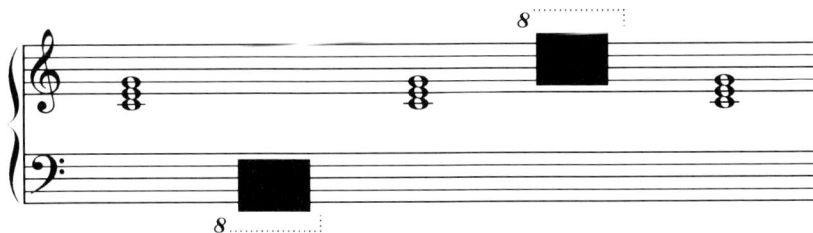

Figure 3

Low clusters should not be played too loudly because they evoke feelings of anxiety in many children. This anxiety usually expresses itself in hostile feelings and refusal to cooperate.

The peekaboo game is effective for children of this age group. They will normally enjoy it; in fact, from a developmental-psychology perspective, this type of game is necessary. Nonetheless, in each lesson or practice session, the game should not be forced on a disinterested child, nor prolonged past the point where the child has become tired of the game.

If the child doesn't respond to the Chord I sound, the teacher must help by beckoning to the animal. If the child presents the animal incorrectly at the sound of a cluster, the teacher must quickly play Chord I again to prevent the child from failing. Once the animal has been selected for Chord I, it must not be changed and must be brought to every lesson.

The parents should repeat this game with their child every day. Soon the child will want to produce the chord on the piano so that the parents can hide the animal.

9

With little hands, Chord I can be played like this:

When the child has become confident in distinguishing Chord I from the clusters, the teacher may introduce Chord II. The teacher instructs the child to bring a new stuffed animal to the next lesson (in addition to the first animal). Chord II can usually be introduced in the third month, or even sooner, but if the child only recognizes Chord I after some delay, it's best to wait and not introduce Chord II too early. One of the main principles of *We Hear and Play* instruction is to avoid hurrying, so that a child has sufficient time for individual progress. Going too fast damages the development of listening and piano-playing skills.

To introduce Chord II, the teacher plays it for the second animal (Figure 4). The child now has to recognize both the I and II chords among the clusters, and this happens most easily when the sounds are part of the peekaboo game.

Occasionally, the child will confuse the I and II chords. When this happens, the teacher should not acknowledge the error, and should continue in a way which avoids calling attention to the error. For example, the teacher may play Chord I as the next sound and immediately beckon to the corresponding animal. If the child makes repeated mistakes, this is a sign that Chord II was introduced too early. If this happens, Chord II must be withdrawn from the game and practice return to Chord I alone.

Withdrawing Chord II is somewhat difficult, because the child will want to continue playing peekaboo with both animals. The teacher can't tell the child they've failed, because in the beginning phase the teacher should use only praise. Some potential solutions are to tell the child the animal has become sick and must stay home, or to ask the second animal if it would like to stay with the teacher that week. In any case, it's better to avoid this problem by introducing Chord II at the right time.

If the child resists learning the second sound, the peekaboo game must be reversed. That is, the child is shown the animal and played the corresponding chord. It's also possible to throw the animal to the child while playing the chord. Different games can be invented for each child, limited only by the teacher's imagination.

Because children often react to failure with hostility and denial, at this stage it's best, for both teacher and parents, to ignore errors and instead respond positively to the next correct answer. When this principle is ignored, the instruction comes to a complete halt. When corrected, a child becomes frustrated and begins to resist. It's often hard for a parent to ignore a child's obvious mistakes; of course, they want their child to demonstrate high achievement. Nevertheless, *the principal task is to not draw attention to the child's mistakes.*

Figure 4

Figure 5

Once a child is able to distinguish the I and II chords effortlessly, the III chord is added in connection with a new stuffed animal (Figure 5). This typically occurs after 6 or 7 months, although it sometimes happens in only 4 months. The same rule applies in any case: before a new chord is introduced, the child must be able to easily recognize the chords they have learned.

If, after 6-8 months, a child can't consistently recognize the I and II chords, the teacher should look for the cause. The most common reasons are weak concentration or poor training at home. Younger children have less ability to concentrate than older children; this means that no aspect of training should be worked for too long, whether ear training, piano playing, or rhythm games. Short, intense training phases, spaced with free play or recovery, are better.

Interested children will want to play the chords themselves, and this is to be encouraged. The chords are most easily played with both hands:

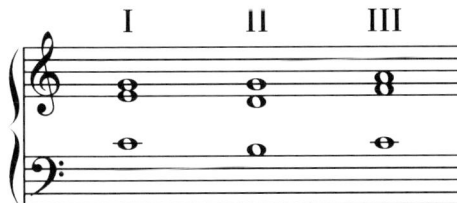

11

The teacher and student can exchange roles; the child plays the chords and the teacher (or parent) plays peekaboo with the stuffed animals. This further expands the game's possibilities and can increase the child's interest in continuing the game.

Once all three chords have been included, the teacher gradually ceases to play interrupting clusters, but plays the three chords in random sequence. In each session, it's a good idea to begin with a different chord so that the child isn't memorizing which one usually comes first. The peekaboo exercises should be repeated daily and reviewed by the teacher in each lesson.

Children are very inventive when playing the peekaboo game with their stuffed animals. They often suggest game variants such as these:

- One child's animals always went to the playground. Before introducing a new sound, the animal had to choose a playground game (slide, swing, merry-go-round).

- Another child didn't want to play peekaboo. Instead, he wanted to tell the teacher what the corresponding animal likes to eat. When the teacher played Chord I, which was a rabbit, the child answered "carrot." For a dog, "bones" was the answer, and for a bear, "honey."

- A girl had discovered that her stuffed animals could slide down the roof of her dollhouse; the mother realized this could be used for the ear training. It was first necessary to slide the animals down the roof to the child when the chords were played. Then, gradually, the sounds were played to the animals directly, and this practice was later integrated with the ball game (which will be explained later). This game variant is well-suited to the beginning phase of ear training. The sliding action is fun for the child and can be seamlessly integrated into the hearing game.

Of course, these game variations can't be imposed on children. A child responds most strongly to self-invented games, because their own games represent their personal preferences. It's best to observe each student in their free time and, from their spontaneous game-playing, filter out useful ideas for their ear-training exercises. Teachers and parents thus have the important task of recognizing the child's signals and applying those signals to the child's musical training.

After a few months, teachers and parents sometimes begin to neglect, or even abandon, the listening exercises. They want to focus entirely on the piano playing. This is not our curriculum. It can lead to the loss of any absolute pitch ability the child has achieved.

Game Two: Ball Playing

Where the peekaboo game provides chord-sound training, the ball game trains the child to hear single pitch sounds. The ball game can be established in the first lesson and used in every lesson and practice session thereafter.

The teacher should have balls in each of the seven colors, available as part of the *We Hear and Play* system. It is good to have a large supply of balls available in the instruction room; about three or four per color is recommended. Obviously, the child must also have balls available at home. An alternative to balls is homemade beanbags, filled with small beans, rice, or cotton. The balls or beanbags must clearly and recognizably correspond to the colors used in *We Hear and Play*.

The goal of the game is that the children will gradually associate the colored balls with the sounds of the colored piano keys.

Figure 6

The game is simple. The child sits on the ground with a supply of balls, and the parent sits some distance away. The child chooses a ball from their supply (Figure 6) and rolls or throws it to the parent. The teacher immediately plays the corresponding pitch in the piano's middle octave (low F through middle G). The teacher may also sing the name of the color at the appropriate pitch. The child may also want to sing along with the name of the color; this is good, but they should not be forced to sing.

This ear training game uses only the colored piano keys shown inside the front cover of *We Hear and Play*. And, of these 9 keys, we use only 7, because F and G occur twice. If the child selects a blue ball, the teacher must play *middle* G. If the child selects orange, the teacher must play *low* F. This is vitally important because doing so clearly marks the upper and lower boundaries. In this beginning phase of ear training, even if the child doesn't hear absolutely, it becomes obvious that blue is the highest sound and orange is the lowest.

<u>This means that low G and middle F are *not* used right away in the ball game.</u> The teacher must follow this rule strictly and explain it clearly to the child's parents.

In each octave, F and G are neighbors and sound similar to each other. By using only middle G and low F, the two notes become easy to tell apart. If a

13

parent at home innocently plays low G and middle F as well, the child may learn that F and G are the same tone.

Additionally, until children become more experienced, they interpret the "same pitch" in different octaves as being different sounds. Using two different octaves for F or G would assign two different sounds to the same ball. Playing two sounds for the same color is confusing, and it is harmful to the instruction process.

Therefore, at this stage of ear training, we will use only the following tones: low F, A, B, middle C, D, E, and G.

The child's imagination should not be restricted, even if they have ideas that challenge the parents' tolerance. Parents often complain that the ball game escalates at home and turns into chaos. This can happen, but for many children the ball game is a way of blowing off steam, and the emotional release is desirable. The child's increased energy can be directed rather than restrained. The child should understand that certain targets are forbidden: a person's face, a fragile object, or a windowpane. Most children laugh when they can hit the parent or teacher; this should be allowed only when there is no danger of injury, such as when soft balls are thrown at the person's back.

Even so, in our multiyear instruction trials using *We Hear and Play*, we learned that aggressive ball-throwing can be hard to handle. The basic rule is that while children need free room, they must be taught to recognize boundaries. Adults set different boundaries for each child, and a teacher must remain flexible. If a teacher makes assumptions like "I will not let a child throw things at me," they may be compelled to change their mind. For example, a very shy child had refused to speak with anyone outside his immediate family, but was able to talk with the teacher after throwing balls at him. This was a big event for all concerned.

Other objects in the instruction room can become a part of the game. A trash can could be a basketball net, or the roof of a doll's house a runway. Variations can always be invented while practicing, and there are certain variations which most children will enjoy (see page 19).

After three months— the earliest instruction duration— the teacher can carefully check to see if the child can hear some single sounds absolutely. Suitable choices are blue (G), red (C), yellow (D), and orange (F). *The first test trial must be approached carefully, without the child's knowledge.* During the ball game, in a short break, the teacher can suddenly play one of these sounds and wait to see how the child reacts. The child may locate the matching ball. If they choose a different ball, it could be due to a lack of concentration, or perhaps the child does not yet hear absolutely. In any case, after the test, the ball game should be continued as usual. A wrong choice should *never* be corrected. At this early stage, the test trial should be conducted by the teacher, never by the parent at home; the parent should continue to practice the game normally. In every case where the parent tested the child, absolute pitch was not achieved. The parent corrected the child by showing which balls to choose, and the child was increasingly disconcerted and finally rejected the balls and sounds completely.

At a certain stage, children will often confuse tones in fifths. For example, a child will hear *green* (E) but guess *purple* (B) which is a fifth above; or they will hear *grey* (A) and guess *yellow* (D) which is a fifth below. This is a good sign that absolute pitch is developing. The fifth interval is the closest relationship between any two musical tones; the child is accurately recognizing this harmonic sound.

Rhythmic training

Because we are training children, we restrict ourselves to elementary tasks and avoid difficult rhythms. Mastering elementary tasks is critically important for all future steps of musical training, but these tasks are often neglected. Our beginning pieces are played to a uniform, steady beat (52 beats per minute). Gradually, playing these regular quarter notes must become habitual.

Parents often wonder: isn't a simple rhythm something ordinary and natural? If a child perceives a steady beat without special training or preparation, why should we take the subject so seriously? Furthermore, with these rhythmic exercises, why are we making the children walk and run? Does this make music instruction into a kind of sports training?

The answer is that, for many children, rhythm is not always innately understood. Furthermore, when they run, children develop a more physical sense of music, which provides an increased feeling for rhythm. Running is directly connected to basic functions of musical instruction. The upcoming chapter will clarify how this works in practice.

Game Three: Running in Time

Human activities almost always consist of a two-stage process: first, perceiving or feeling; and second, turning perception into expression. In a child's musical development we begin at the first stage by promoting their perception of rhythm.

This is how the running game works: as the child runs, the teacher plays a steady rhythm using Chord I (the I-III chords are found in *We Hear and Play* Volume 1, page 5). The right hand plays the combined chord (C, E, and G) while the left hand plays bass notes in the same rhythm. The bass notes must be only C, or C and G, as in this example.

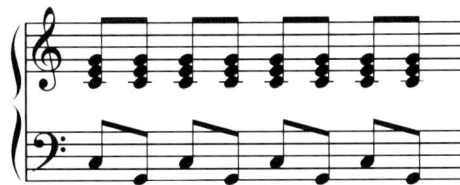

The teacher should repeat the chord at each of the child's steps. The speed should be adapted to the child's pace. It will probably be rather fast, since a child usually runs quickly. It is important that the child runs with feeling, internally participating with the music.

This game should be introduced in the first session. Initially, the teacher must prompt the child to begin running, then adjust their chord playing to the child's steps. Without being instructed, the child will gradually understand— sometimes in the first session, often in subsequent sessions— that during these chord games they should listen attentively and run in rhythm.

It is part of our methodical procedure to repeat the C-major tonic sound often. Through this repetition the child always hears this chord better than others, and this is one of the prerequisites to absolute pitch development. This repetition also provides psychological security, because the child hears this "instruction sound" enough to develop an internal relationship to it during the course of the lessons.

The teacher or parent should never try to use different chords to make the game "more interesting," even though we find different chords interesting as adults. Two changing chords, or any similar alterations, will confuse the child, even if the chords are played separately as in this example:

Similarly, chord sequences with modulations or expansions sound comfortable to adults, but they ignore the goal of this instruction and of music training in general; teachers and parents should avoid them in the best interest of the child.

After the child is introduced to Chord II in the peekaboo game, this chord can also be used in this rhythm game, although it should not yet be used together with Chord I. In this case, the bass notes can be either a repeated G, or G and D alternating, as in this example:

This also applies to the III chord. At an advanced level, when the child can follow the change of a chord, the teacher may change chords, provided that each new chord is repeated enough times to be distinct, as in this example:

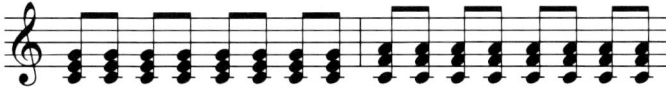

The child can respond to the change of sounds with a change of movement. Here are some examples.

1. The child runs normally to Chord I, and holds their treble hand (right hand) up high during Chord II.

2. With Chord I the child runs in one direction, and with Chord II the other.

If there is a table in the instruction room, the child can run around it, which is more fun. The teacher's piano can serve the same purpose if placed in the middle of the room. Otherwise the child can run around other objects, like chairs.

It's better to play this game in a large room. The child feels more free, and less physically cramped, and can move quickly and urgently.

With these exercises, rhythm becomes clearer and harmonic perception improves. Combining rhythm and harmony helps develop the correct feeling for both; the musical structure together with visceral response fosters the close connection between rhythm and harmony.

Game Four: Clapping and Stomping

Another part of the training is clapping practice. This should be practiced often. The teacher and child sit facing each other, at a height so that both can comfortably touch each other's palms.

Version 1: The teacher repeats "One, two," rhythmically, at a moderate speed (69 beats per minute). On "one," the teacher and child clap each other's hands, and on "two" they clap their own hands. Obviously, this game must be made interesting and fun.

Version 2: The teacher repeats "one, two, three", at the same speed as in Version One.

On "one," the teacher and child each clap their partner's hands (Figure 7);

on "two," they clap their own hands (Figure 8);

on "three," they each clap their hands against their thighs (Figure 9).

Figure 7

Version 3: The teacher and the child stand face to face. The teacher counts "one, two, three," as in Version Two.

On "one," both clap the partner's hands;

on "two," each stomp one foot;

on "three," each stomp their other foot.

Figure 8

The teacher should observe the child to make sure they consistently use the same leg for "two." The teacher, standing opposite the child, should move as a mirror image.

These clapping games must be repeated in each instructional session and every day at home. Game variants are acceptable.

Sometimes, for physical or psychological reasons, children don't want to clap, but will cooperate with stomping. These rhythm games can be redesigned to be played with stomping or with simple percussion instruments.

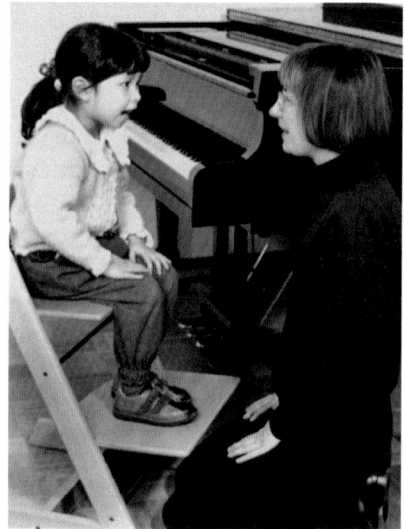
Figure 9

Additional Listening Games

Ball game variations

Tube game: Children love to send objects through tubes. An object's disappearance at one end and reappearance at the other end can seem magical. An exciting variation of the ball game is to take a long cardboard tube, wide enough for the balls to fit into, and fasten it to a stand which has a downward slope (Figure 10). A tube for mailing posters is usually a good size; appropriate tubes may also be found inside rolls of wrapping paper.

Figure 10

The child selects a ball and inserts it into the tube. The teacher plays the associated tone at the moment when the child chooses the ball. Alternately, children often enjoy hiding the ball from the teacher before dropping it into the tube; in which case, the teacher plays the tone when the ball emerges from the end of the tube (Figure 11). The teacher may also cut tops off of plastic bottles, such as milk jugs or juice bottles, and place them at the end of the tube. This usually fascinates children, and they will watch carefully to see if the ball falls into the bottle. When the ball drops into the bottle, the teacher can play the tone again. When one bottle is filled, another may be placed beneath the tube.

Just for fun, or perhaps to play a joke on the teacher, children may insert pencils, toys, and other small objects into the tube, or they may try to insert many balls as quickly as possible. When this happens, the teacher doesn't need to keep up with the child's speed and play all the tones, but may allow the child to play the game for fun and relaxation. It is a good activity for hand coordination and body movement.

Figure 11

19

The tube itself can become an entertaining toy. It can be spoken through, listened with, or reached into. It's fun to wave around, to grab at, to hit with, and to throw. This kind of play builds the child's relationship with the tube and further encourages them to play ear training games with the tube.

Bottle game: The plastic bottles from the tube game may be arranged lying down against a wall, so that the child can roll balls into their open tops. The tone may be played when the ball is chosen or when it successfully enters the bottle (or both). Boys usually enjoy this game more than girls.

Cloth game: Another ball game variation is to use a scarf or cloth spread out on the floor. The child hides a ball underneath, and the teacher tries to guess which color has been hidden. When the cloth is lifted, the teacher plays the ball's tone. The teacher may hide other colored objects beneath the cloth, and the child must guess by reaching underneath and touching the objects; this is more difficult, because the child has to remember a specific object as well as its color, but it can be good training for the child's tactile sense.

Guessing game: The child can throw the ball at the teacher's back and play its tone, and the teacher can guess which ball it is. When the child can hear absolutely, the game may be reversed so that that the child guesses the tones.

All ball game variations can be played with role reversal, so that the teacher (or parent) plays with the balls and the child plays or sings the tones.

Take-away game

Once the child is able to identify red and blue relatively well, the teacher can introduce the "take-away" game. The child sits on the ground; the teacher puts several blue balls near the child's right hand, and several red balls near the left. The teacher then says, "I'm going to play blue" and prompts the child to remove a blue ball. Next the teacher tells the child to figure out which ball to take away and plays red. Normally this is easy for the child. If the teacher sees the child hesitating, they can let a stuffed animal or hand puppet make the choice for the child.

After 6 to 12 months, children should hear all seven sounds absolutely, with no errors. Nonetheless, some sounds may be less familiar than others, and the take-away game can strengthen their recognition of these less well-known sounds. The teacher shows the child two colored balls: one representing a well-known sound, and the other a less-familiar sound. The teacher plays the well-known sound, and the child takes away the corresponding ball. Then the teacher replaces the missing ball with another well-known color, and plays the less familiar sound. Because there are only two balls to choose from, one of which is familiar, the child picks the correct one by the process of elimination. In time this game can be expanded to three balls.

The teacher and student can exchange roles in most of the listening games. In the take-away game, for example, the child can play the sounds on the piano while the teacher or parent selects the correct ball. The teacher can sometimes select an incorrect ball to test the child's concentration and hearing ability.

Hearing games require high concentration which leads to fatigue. Teachers should plan the instruction with variety in mind, and remember to keep time limits. When a child becomes tired of a game, a teacher should respect this and immediately declare a break.

Imitation game

If a teacher has two equally tuned pianos in the instruction room, they can play the "imitation game" with the student. The teacher plays a low cluster on one piano; the child repeats it on the other. The teacher continues to play various clusters in different places on the keyboard. Since the child knows how to play Chord I, the teacher should use it in the game as well. The teacher may begin to play single sounds as well, specifically red (C), blue (G), or yellow (D). The child often finds the correct key. The teacher must praise each of the child's imitations, whether or not it matches the teacher's notes, because it's enough for the child to be ready and willing to play the game.

Guidance for Teachers

Suggested First Lesson

Here is a representative first lesson to help a teacher plan and carry out a child's introduction to *We Hear and Play*. Because the training is highly individualized, there may be times when this suggested procedure can't be followed.

1. Introduce the Teacher to the Child

The teacher must first establish rapport with the child. Before teaching a child of this age, the teacher must make good human contact. Naturally, the parents must help motivate the child for instruction and encourage the child's interest in the teacher, but this cannot replace effective communication between teacher and child. It is good if the child brings one or more of their favorite games to the first lesson; this helps inform the teacher of the child's interests.

Also, the teacher should have toys, paper, crayons, and picture books in the instruction room. (See "Using Additional Instructional Material", page 34.) These items have two important functions. First, since all children are familiar with toys, this helps them feel at home. Second, if the child is unable to cooperate with the piano instruction (for whatever reasons), the teacher can play with the child using an instructional toy. This helps stave off the parents' concern that, in a paid lesson, no learning is occurring. The toys can be used at any stage of training; sometimes children won't be able to concentrate and learn, or they will need a rest between instruction phases. The child's need for phases of game-playing should become obvious to the parents.

If it's hard to make contact, picture books are often helpful. As the teacher reads or tells the stories, the child becomes more accessible.

2. Create Association Between Stuffed Animal and Chord I

In any case, the child brings a favorite stuffed animal to the first lesson. This animal will always be used in connection with Chord I (as described in the Peekaboo Game on page 8). The child is told that the chord is the sound of their favorite animal. It is critical that Chord I should never be played in other octaves. The parents should be encouraged to participate in the peekaboo game; this game usually is great fun for the child and the entire family.

3. Introduce "Bass Hand" and "Treble Hand"

For preschool children, the labels "right" and "left" are abstract and easily confused. We use the terms "bass hand" and "treble hand" instead. The *We*

Hear and Play piano books are arranged so that bass pieces are printed on the left pages and treble pieces are printed on the right pages, so a child will understand which hand to use from their own body's orientation.

The teacher opens Book 1 to pages 6 and 7 and places it in front of the child's body (on the floor, table, or piano). The teacher can now bring his own hands, or the child's hands, to each page in turn, speaking the words "bass hand" and "treble hand." The child, or the stuffed animal, can repeat these words if they want to.

If the child is agreeable, the bass and treble clefs can be drawn on their respective hands with a non-toxic, washable felt-tip pen. Alternately, the teacher may touch each of the child's hands to show which is which; if the child refuses to allow this, the teacher must express the distinction verbally. The closer their relationship becomes, the easier it is for the teacher to communicate the instructional material to the child (see also "Step by Step Guidance," page 35).

After this introduction, the teacher may show page 6 or 7 to the child and encourage the child to raise the corresponding hand. If the child raises the opposite hand, the teacher should not correct the child, but instead respond positively by showing the symbol that the child has indicated.

These games should be practiced daily at home. It is usually better to have multiple short practice sessions, distributed throughout the day, than to have a single lengthy session.

A three-year-old's attention is generally exhausted after these two games. The session should end with a different activity, one the child prefers. The teacher might offer the child a small prize for "good cooperation," preferably in one of the colors from the ball game.

4. Introduce "Purple" and "Yellow" Notes

With older children (4-4½), the teacher determines in each case whether, in the first lesson, the student can attempt to learn and play one or two sounds. If so, the teacher opens Book 1 to page 8 and 9 and asks the child which hand they would like to play first. Using their preferred hand, the child can find on the page the "bass hand" or "treble hand" symbol. They can point at the symbol and find the first note next to it (purple or yellow). Usually the child will point with their index finger, which is the finger that will play the note. The teacher can now place a purple or yellow sticker on the B or D key, and the child will be able to play their first note on the piano. For easier coordination of finger and key, the child may want to have their fingernail colored with purple or yellow nail polish.

If it seems desirable, the other note (yellow or purple) can be introduced in the same manner.

With these two tones, we can already make music. The same tone can be played twice, or three times; the two different notes can be played simultaneously or alternately. The child can play one tone while the teacher (or stuffed animal) plays the other (see also "Step by Step Guidance," page 35).

Depending on the child's interests, steps 3 and 4 could be replaced by the rhythm game (see page 15) or the ball game (see page 13).

Piano Training Fundamentals

Basic Positioning Using Middle C

In *basic positioning*, the student is given a "home position" for each hand. Each finger is assigned to a specific key, and each finger plays only its assigned key. This develops the solidarity between the finger, the key, and the sound, which makes fingering the instrument more natural and familiar.

Without a solidly learned basic position, a child is permanently unsteady. As they continue to practice, their sense of fingering grows proportionately bad, and their uncertainty becomes recognizable. In short, lack of basic fingering position can do great harm to a child's musicianship.

Therefore, any piano training must first settle on a basic position. In the 19th century, the left hand was placed on middle C through G while the right hand played high C through G. However, since the beginning of the 20th century, pianists have used the centralized middle C, in which each thumb plays middle C while the other fingers play the higher or lower keys. All the C-major pitches are thereby included, which is a great advantage both for piano instruction and absolute pitch training. This is one of the primary reasons why we use this basic position in *We Hear and Play*. With it, children can quickly play many songs; plus, since the white keys are also used in G-major and F-major, it allows the timely and meaningful introduction of B-flat and F-sharp.

Attack Quality and Sound Quality

Hearing and controlling the piano's sound quality is a more subtle process than it is with other instruments. Wind and string instruments can obviously be manipulated by the musician's posture, playing style, or technique to change sound character, dynamics, and tone color. By contrast, the piano's sound quality is difficult to detect. Each piano has its certain characteristic sound which can't be changed. Nevertheless, a standard, normally tuned piano will respond to different approaches, producing different sound character and, therefore, different sound quality.

A child being trained with *We Hear and Play* should have a piano that is in good condition (see "Materials You Will Need" on page 4), but a good piano doesn't have to be expensive. What is important is that the mechanics of the piano are correctly regulated so that the effort required to press the keys is neither too heavy nor too light, and so that the instrument has a standard key depth. The tone color and sound strength should be uniform across the board, and the sound should not be too sharp or too soft. Tuning is indispensable, but a piano may be well tuned and still fail these other requirements.

This section describes the "good" or "pretty" piano sound, discussed in terms of sound and sound quality. These expressions are basically equivalent, but with shades of difference.

When we refer to a "good sound" in *We Hear and Play*, we mean principally that a child plays at an average volume. From this, a good sound emerges if

1. The sound has substance, which arises from flexible physical and psychological bearing.

2. In the attack, the sound of the finger or fingernail pushing against the key is avoided, and releasing the key does not create a sound from the mechanics of the piano. (This consideration is often ignored.)

When a scale is played, a good sound quality fulfills these conditions:

1. The notes are played legato.

2. Rhythmic playing is accomplished, with all sounds of equal length.

3. All sounds have the same volume, controlled by the child's active listening and emotional involvement.

It is extremely important that the child learns to play all pieces with a fluid, legato motion, but they should not be encouraged to play too quickly.

Deviations should be avoided from the start, as they reduce sound quality. For example, a child may play all or part of a piece too strongly or weakly. In extreme cases, they may drop notes entirely, or add delays which allow the music to become arrhythmic.

It's not enough merely to avoid negative factors. One would think that avoiding negative habits leads to improved skill, but avoidance is a passive approach. To achieve higher quality, seek active improvements. Although we are only at the beginning level of piano playing, we are already in a sphere in which two control elements— rational intellect and instinctive emotion— cooperate in many ways. If the teacher continues to improve and refine their own perception of beautiful sound, they will achieve the best results when they are able to transfer their developed perception to a child through the instructional sessions.

To ensure a good attack:

1. The fingertip must not be stiff. Rather, the energy necessary for the attack should come from the body, transmitted from the shoulder and upper arm in a gradual, wavelike motion. The teacher should demonstrate this and explain it in a manner appropriate to the child.

2.   The middle of the key should be pressed. Children often want to press the right or left side and thus touch the adjacent key. This touch feels comfortable and secure, and can easily become habit. A child's need for security, however, should be satisfied with good human contact between teacher and child, and by honest praise for earnest effort.

3.   When playing white keys, the fingers should not stray into the upper area of the key (near the black keys). This is a typical habit which also develops from a need for security. Once this habit has been established, it is hard to correct. The upper areas of the white keys should only be used when they are needed: when alternating quickly between black and white keys, or when using multiple black keys in a chord. These situations do not occur in elementary stages (such as *We Hear and Play*). When the white keys' upper areas are pressed, the attack energy is not optimally used, and is partially lost. If this habit is left uncorrected, a child can develop the feeling that only blunt sounds come from the instrument, and may therefore perceive these blunt sounds as good sounds. This bad impression should be stopped before it starts.

4.   Finger posture for little hands.

Finger posture for children should be assessed individually, according to their physical state. Nevertheless, the most common approach is this:

- With the index, middle, and ring finger: first flatly, and then, after some time, roundly.

- With the thumb: use the side of the thumb. The child may first attempt to use the tip of the thumb, since they have been taught to use the tips of their other fingers, but the side should be used. Furthermore, the teacher must ensure that the child forms a straight line from the wrist to the tip of the thumb. Initially, the second joint of the thumb may bend, but this is not a problem, as this joint later becomes stable.

- With the pinkie: first flatly, like the other fingers, and then gradually slightly round, so that the first and second finger joints are not bent back.

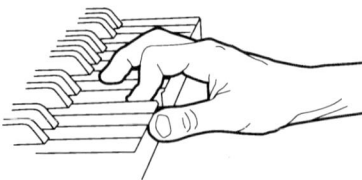

Figure 12

Figure 13

Piano educators are trained to know that finger joints must not be snapped. Many children are biased toward bending their finger joints backwards as they press down (Figure 12), and often this bias seems impossible to correct. These children, who have innately weak and yielding joints, should hold their fingers flat before each attack to use their hand's grasping movement and its inherent energy. The teacher should also have the child do a practice exercise which strengthens the muscles and tendons of the finger and hand: pressing the surface of a white key firmly and continuously while drawing the finger towards the body. This exercise causes finger posture to gradually become round (Figure 13). The exercise should be repeated with each finger, as it is helpful for all four fingers.

Gradual Approach to Steady Rhythm

The steady rhythm in the clapping and running games should also be actively expressed in the child's piano playing. This doesn't happen immediately. The teacher must patiently guide the child's initially unbalanced playing into a rhythmic state. Here are a few important instructions.

1. *We Hear and Play* Volume One features pieces which require attention to rhythm (#69-106, for example). When the child is playing these numbers, the teacher should point at the notes with a pencil or small stick, using a rhythmic movement (Figure 14). The parent should imitate this at home.

Figure 14

2. Initially, the child may play notes out of rhythm because they are not yet able to quickly produce the note with the appropriate finger. This cognitive process takes a different amount of time for each child, but reaction time is always improved through daily practicing. Their playing will become rhythmic only if appropriate guidance is given during the practice sessions.

27

3. The connection between the printed note and its assigned finger is one of the most elementary technical bases. It is important for the child's entire future musicianship. This connection develops especially well at this age, and the teacher should give the highest priority to developing this skill. This is only possible if the session is made fun for the child.

4. The teacher should never use abstract words like *rhythmic* or *steady* because the children won't understand them. Learning rhythm must be a natural, unconscious process.

5. For success in rhythmic playing, the child must become able to play a piece fluently, without stopping. It is dangerously easy to practice with stops and starts. To avoid this, it is best to let the child keep their own time while reading the notes. It is bad habit to play a wrong note, notice this, stop, and then begin again somewhere. Once this practice becomes habit, musical rhythm will not develop. The teacher must prevent this habit from forming.

There are many reasons why a child may play with interruptions, including

1. The teacher does not notice the child is stopping.

2. The difference between playing with and without stopping is too subtle for an inexperienced teacher to recognize.

3. The teacher is not aware of the serious negative effects that playing with stops will have on further development.

4. The teacher has no strategy for preventing this bad habit.

5. The teacher sees the problem, but does not want to destroy the child's interest in playing the piano, and so lets the problem continue. Perhaps they do not expect that a child of this age is capable of playing without stopping.

How does the stopping begin to occur? Here are some typical causes:

1. *At home the child practices infrequently or not at all.*

   Some parents do not concern themselves with their child's musical development and therefore do not practice with the child. Some parents don't attend lessons and so have no idea of the correct procedure. Other parents do attend but pay no attention. The children of such parents will not be properly guided at home.

2. *The teacher does not point out the notes or does not do so correctly.*

   Pointing out the notes is an essential component of the instruction. When the teacher does not take control of this process, for whatever reason, the child cannot play fluently without stopping.

3. *The child practices frequently and diligently but always plays with stopping.*

    The stoppage becomes programmed into the child's behavior. Unfortunately, practice is often too fast. The child's pace of learning must be accommodated, and the child should be allowed to practice slowly— and with great patience. Naturally, patience is also expected of the teacher and parents.

4. *The child does not connect the printed notes with the imagined sound developed by absolute pitch.*

    Stopping will occur more often if the child is unable to imagine the note's sound. They should be guided so that the use of the gradually developed and consolidated absolute pitch becomes habit in their playing.

Fluent, stop-free playing contributes to the development of a good rhythmic feeling in the same way as if the child were dancing. With stopping, even an existing feel for rhythm will develop more slowly, or may be suppressed altogether.

For development of a good rhythmic feeling, it is important that the child plays partly from memory, but not completely from memory. The child should always have the notes before their eyes, even if they are playing from memory. This enhances their ability to imagine the note sounds prior to pressing each key.

If a child plays a piece entirely from memory, without looking at the notes, the danger exists that they will play entirely from memorized hand movements; this renders the child's internal representation of the sound— which is their developing absolute pitch— unnecessary. *The danger of this situation cannot be taken too seriously*, especially since it's not always obvious that the child is playing from physical memory. Experience has shown that even pianists with absolute pitch will memorize hand movements if poorly instructed. Playing from physical memory leads to a musical dead end.

Fortunately, there are concrete signs that can help teachers detect this problem. Perhaps the child can play a piece only from the beginning and never in the middle. Or an advanced student, who does not imagine the note sounds properly and has therefore practiced incorrectly, may play strangely, choosing either notes which are harmonious to the melody or notes which are not even part of the piece.

Although this may seem unrelated to rhythm, the different training tasks are closely connected. It should be apparent that even if a child can play fluently and rhythmically, "turned off" internal listening is undesirable, and should be actively avoided. A child who can play well from memory is often referred to as "gifted" or "a musical child," but in reality, this habit can be the start of a chain of negative habits.

Short and Long Notes

In *We Hear and Play* the first pieces that develop rhythmic feeling and expression use two quarter notes and one half note. These begin with Vol. 1, #69.

When playing a half note, the child should mark its second beat by hitting their foot loudly against the stool (Figure 15). We call this beat a "Stomper" and indicate it with a triangle symbol. Longer notes require additional Stompers: a dotted half note needs two Stompers, and a whole note uses three Stompers. Because the Stomper is an element for developing rhythm, it must be done at the same tempo as the previous quarter notes.

In practice, this isn't as easy as it sounds. A child will, at first, stomp as quickly as possible— particularly with the whole notes, which have three Stompers after the key is pressed (#109), and with the dotted half-note which has two Stompers (#113).

The teacher must somehow slow down

Figure 15

these fast Stompers into an integrated rhythm. The child must first have practiced the piece well, so they have good control of the notes and can play with confidence. Only then can the teacher say, "I would like to march to your music" or "May I clap when you play this piece?" With an adept gesture or interruption, the teacher can draw the child's attention to the moment right before the Stompers, so that the child stomps naturally and rhythmically.

Stomping is more effective than conventional instruction. Ordinarily, a teacher attempts to enforce correct tempo and rhythm through loud counting, which the child is supposed to follow. But when the child stomps the rhythm instead, it is connected to the movement of a body part; furthermore, each movement carries a physical shock. This impresses the rhythm directly into the child's active consciousness.

Children who don't want to stomp, or who are too small to do it, are discussed later (see page 41), but children are usually willing and able to stomp on the stool. The Stomper is discussed further in the commentary for pieces #66-68.

Although the stomping should be in the same rhythm as the previous notes, and produced with the utmost discipline, the rhythm doesn't have to be as unwavering as a metronome. The regularity in music recognized as "rhythmic" is not so rigid. The teacher should strive not for precision, but for the highest rhythmic quality. This means avoiding inaccuracy in sustaining longer notes and rests, or carelessness during advanced stages of development; these destroy the kernel and structure of the art. A bias towards careless playing should be heavily corrected in older students.

If the student makes mindful choices in sustaining notes and rests, this habit becomes an advantage in later life— whether they play often or rarely, on whatever instrument, in whichever style.

Training Preschool Children

A preschool child rarely has a natural drive toward piano instruction. The decision to play a musical instrument is usually made by the parents. If it is left to the child, by the time they are capable of making such a decision they will have lost the most important years for musical development.

In this book we show how important it is to have an early start to develop certain musical abilities. We hope that, in the future, more parents will begin musical instruction with their infants. The problem for most teachers, aside from methodological questions, is that they have had too little experience in teaching preschool children. The following thoughts may help.

Interacting with Children

The teacher's first and most important task is to make good contact with the child. A preschool child will learn only if they have a positive emotional relationship with the teacher. Because many children are afraid to be left alone with a strange person, a parent's presence is initially important. As the child becomes more comfortable, the parent may leave the room for part of the lesson, so the child doesn't feel like the parent is monitoring.

A child's attention span is short. It usually lasts only until they satisfy a direct curiosity or the prospect for a reward. Their interest can last a long time if they perceive the activity as pleasurable, but we must always keep in mind that children communicate with their surroundings by playing. It is through playing that children gain their understanding of not only tangible objects but also social behavior.

The child's greatest reward in learning comes through success or affirmation. With babies, this happens mostly through physical responses (smiling or petting). As a child grows older, these are replaced by verbal affirmations. A further, important form of reward is the appreciation and care of the person to whom the child relates most closely.

Besides this, imitation and identification are of the greatest importance. A child's ability to learn by observation is essential in this type of education. This learning is critical to the child's developing personality, as it imprints lasting patterns of behavior. A child will imitate people with whom they have a positive relationship and with whom they can identify.

The teacher should strive for

- Building and maintaining positive emotional contact with the child

- Interest in the child's personality, not merely their achievements

- Good contact with the parents, with agreement on essential points and readiness for dialogue.

To promote independence, the teacher should encourage and strengthen the child's efforts. The adult should step in to help only if the child is unable to solve a problem on their own. Having independent behavior encouraged at the infant age is a prerequisite for personality development, as it allows the child to exercise optimally all their faculties for interaction with the world.

Teachers and parents must never forget that game playing, and learning by playing, should be given the highest precedence when working with an infant.

All children depend on success and approval. They want to be praised for achievement. Otherwise, they lose their patience and the desire to achieve, and learning problems will appear. The younger the child, the more important it is to have direct approval. Only through strengthened self-confidence can a child find delight in their learning.

Many parents, especially those who are themselves teachers, expect the child to discover their own interest in music. But such a discovery is not possible for this age group. The love of the work develops in proportion to the love for the teacher. Approval from teacher and parents is the next most important factor.

A child's biological rhythms fluctuate between periods of high energy and relaxation. For instruction, this means that phases of activity must be followed by phases of rest. The teacher must include well-planned breaks in the teaching session and make sure the activity being attempted is appropriate to the child's physical and emotional condition.

Over the weeks and months of instruction, certain rituals will establish themselves. For example, one child may start each lesson by playing the peekaboo game and then stop to read a book. If the teacher responds to the child's requests, they will be able in turn to make requests of the child; so the child's needs are incorporated into the teaching process. A person who wishes to work with children must come to the child's level and accept the child as an equal partner.

The teacher and parents must understand that learning freely is more pleasurable than learning by compulsion. Certainly, there are constraints, as the child is given a choice of activities from a menu. But the child can determine the sequence of activity; for example, rhythm clapping, then piano playing, then ball throwing. Giving a child freedom in learning does not mean the teacher should let children do anything they want. That would make instruction meaningless.

There are no universal rules regulating interaction with young children. But the teacher who is involved in each lesson, allowing the child to express their own developing personality, will find joy and success in their teaching.

Using We Hear and Play

How to Use the Looseleaf Format

The looseleaf format is helpful for several reasons.

1.   Heavy piano books are difficult for small children to manage. With a looseleaf system they can carry to their lesson only those pages they really need.

2.   Children are often not very careful with books, and the books fall from the piano and are damaged. The looseleaf format avoids this.

3.   There are longer songs which require several pages. The process of turning the pages of a bound book often causes rhythmic problems. Looseleaf pages may be placed next to each other and turned quickly.

4. The teacher may keep most of the piano book, and give the student only the new pages for each lesson.

This may seem restrictive, but it is very practical. We experimented with this process for many years. If the teacher gives the student only the pages for their daily practice, the student will normally accept them without any trouble. But if the student has the entire book, they will often want to reject the teacher's selections and make their own choices. This can be counterproductive, because children are not able to judge the difficulty of a piece— but if a teacher refuses to accept the child's preference, this can cause frustration and disappointment. This becomes the beginning of an endless and meaningless struggle. Therefore, we think it is better to avoid such problems from the start.

The process can, in fact, be a very positive experience. As the child continues to receive more new pages in each lesson, they will be happy to see their book "growing up."

5. The teacher may arrange the order of piano pieces to support a child's individual progress.

Although the order of pieces in Book I should not be altered, from Book II onwards the teacher may reorder the pieces to accommodate each student's individual needs. Some children may need more etudes, like the Beyer pieces, and others will prefer to play songs. Some children may have problems playing with both hands. For these and many other reasons, the teacher may want to rearrange the pieces to best help the student learn and grow.

Using Additional Instructional Material

A preschool child usually won't be able to concentrate on musical things for an entire lesson, so the teacher should have other training materials available. These should be designed for short-term use, so that the main instruction can be easily returned to. Examples of game materials that use the *We Hear and Play* colors are

- Wax crayons and paper (non-toxic crayons or pencils are recommended)

- Puzzle balls with pieces that fit through matching slots

- Jigsaw puzzles of animals and fairy-tale scenes

- Spinning tops in each of the *We Hear and Play* colors. Spinning a top also promotes finger coordination.

- Origami paper for folding

- Hand puppets. All children love puppets. They are good for role playing, and a child can identify with them. In team piano playing a child often enjoys it when the teacher plays piano by using the puppets.

- Wooden building blocks to which grey and purple are added (these colors are usually missing from normal sets of colored blocks).

- Little wooden animals in the *We Hear and Play* colors

- Strings with large beads in the *We Hear and Play* colors

- Picture books, preferably without too much text. These may be partially suited for the listening exercises. The teacher may play sounds which match the colors in a picture.

- Balls. A set of seven balls is available in the *We Hear and Play* colors. For instruction, we recommend a ball supply of four to five balls per color. The more that are available, the more meaningfully they can be used. Parents should also have more than one set of these colored balls.

Step-by-step Guidance for the Musical Pieces

The next three sections correspond to the three *We Hear and Play* piano books. Each piece in the *We Hear and Play* books is discussed, to explain both how the piece is integrated with the instructional method and how it contributes to the child's training in absolute pitch, rhythm, and performance quality. Naturally, there is conceptual overlap between these explanations and the instructions which have already been given. Although this commentary guides the instructor, it isn't meant to replace the teacher's own initiative.

Volume One

Pages:

6-7   In the very first lesson the child is introduced to the terms "bass hand" and "treble hand." We avoid the words "clef," "left hand," and "right hand," which are all too abstract for a 3- or 4-year-old child. When the teacher shows the child both bass and treble hands, they must not sit facing the child, or the child will be confused by the teacher's hands being on opposite sides.

The teacher shows page 7 to the child and explains that this sign means "bass hand." The teacher should touch the child's hand to make a physical connection with the symbol. The "treble hand" is introduced in the same way. Once both hands are identified, the child should touch each hand to the corresponding symbol on page 6 or 7.

A child will learn most easily when the symbols are drawn on the corresponding hands, so that they can compare the hands to the pages. Most children will allow the teacher to draw on their hands, but the teacher should always ask the child's permission. The teacher should also let the child select a color to draw the sign with. If the child doesn't want the symbols drawn on their hands, the teacher must respect this, and the parents must not pressure the child to accept the drawings. There are lots of other ways to introduce the labels "bass hand" and "treble hand" in everyday life; for instance, by applying the symbols to gloves or shoes.

It usually takes only a short while for children between 3-4½ to correctly associate both hands. When playing the piano, they occasionally confuse the two, but this tendency fades during the first year of instruction. If a child continues to confuse their hands, this could represent a problem with left-right coordination, which would probably become evident later, when the child plays piano with both hands.

35

8-9 #1-2: The teacher shows the child the purple note or the yellow note. For each note, the child looks for the corresponding key (marked with a same-colored dot) and plays it. If the child doesn't use the correct finger, the teacher shows how to use the index finger (Figure 16). Typically, children enjoy using purple or yellow nail polish to color the fingernail of each index finger.

Because the child has not played piano before, it's important to start with correct finger posture and attack position (see page 24).

Figure 16

Figure 17

Figure 18

With children, verbal explanations and lectures are the *least* effective way to do this. They should be taught by touch. To accomplish this, the teacher may stroke the child's finger, from its middle to the tip, while bringing the finger into a good posture (Figure 17). The teacher can also help by holding the child's fingertip between their thumb and index finger and pressing the key together with the child (Figure 18).

Then the child can try to press the key by themselves, without help, while the teacher points at the notes with a pencil. Children should press the front part of the key, which requires less force than the back of the key. Only later, when the black keys are used, it will become necessary to press the white keys towards the back.

10-11   #3-4: These notes are low A and middle E, which are "grey" and "green" respectively. They should be played with the middle finger of each hand. These notes should be introduced no earlier than the second lesson. Although from an adult's perspective this learning is extremely simple, it's better to train a child in these small steps.

12-13   #5-6: For the first time the child plays two notes in sequence, using the same hand. The teacher or parent should *always* point at the notes with a pencil when the child is playing. Pointing at the notes will teach the child to read notes from left to right, without having to explain "left" and "right." Pointing helps the child stay oriented and not get confused about which notes have and haven't been played yet.

The notes can be played at their normal walking speed. A slow speed is desirable (63 beats per minute).

Children often check to see that they have played the notes correctly. They look down at their fingers on the keys; then, when they look back at the page, they lose their place. Many children keep this habit even after years of training; if so, the teacher and parents must continue to help by pointing at the notes.

Although a child will usually play non-legato, many children can smooth out the notes after the teacher provides an example. The teacher may also place their fingers loosely on the child's fingers, to play the sounds together, so that the child begins to feel how as one finger leaves a key, the next one presses down. Additionally, introducing a swaying or swinging movement can help the child feel the process of connecting the sounds. Girls often show more skill at this than boys do.

14-15   #7-8: Children often think that these are identical to #5-6. Once they play the notes, they realize that the other finger plays first. Again, it helps if the teacher or parent points from above at the notes to be played.

If the child can already connect both notes, they should be repeated consecutively. This is good finger training. Also, the teacher can run while the child repeats these notes. The child, watching the teacher, has fun trying different playing speeds, to see the teacher run slowly or quickly.

"Who can play longest?" is another game which uses these two notes. The teacher plays the note repetition softly, in a higher or lower octave (or on a second piano). After a few seconds the teacher asks the child: can you play longer than that? They play together for a while, after which the teacher can say, "I can't hold out much longer!" and forfeit the game. The child is happy to win, and may continue for some time just to prove their superiority. Sometimes, also, a child announces "I played longer and won!" Naturally, the teacher should accept this and praise the child for their endurance.

Another game is to put pieces of colored paper on the ground. Alternating with either grey/purple or green/yellow, the pieces can be placed at a distance from each other that matches the child's stride. While the teacher plays the notes, the child runs on the corresponding colors. This game is good for rhythmic training and absolute pitch development.

The teacher can create simple improvisations (with either a soft bass or sonorous descant melody) while the child continues to play pieces #7-8. The teacher must be careful to maintain a subtle presence when doing this, because the child will become upset if their own part is drowned out.

16-19	**#9-12:** Three-note practice using these now well-known sounds.
20-21	**#13-14:** The sounds "blue" (G) and "orange" (F) are introduced, to be played with the ring finger of the respective hand. The sounds are introduced in the same manner as the previous ones.
22-33	**#15-26:** These are all the different combinations of the notes learned so far. Children can use these pieces as their weekly homework. Although they may appear simple to an adult, they should be practiced thoroughly. When practicing, children generally want to play a piece only once, rather than repeat it, so these pages offer many different pieces at the same degree of difficulty. It's important not to skip pieces or move forward too quickly. Training for piano, listening, and rhythm should all develop in parallel.
34-35	**#27-28:** The thumb on red (C) presses the key in a different position than any of the other fingers. Children typically try to press the key with the flat tip of the thumb. We recommend that the teacher manually bring the child's hand into the correct attack position (Figures 19-20), and initially help the child play this note. If the child refuses this approach, one of the stuffed animals may speak to the thumb, perhaps to ask the thumb if it would please lay on its side.

Figure 19   Figure 20

Sometimes the thumb position must be corrected again, even after a great deal of training.

36-47   #29-40: These pages are similar to #15-26, providing different combinations of the notes used so far.

48-49   #41-42: The pinkie finger needs special attention. It is smaller and weaker than the other fingers, and is used far less frequently in daily life. At this point in the instruction it's best if this finger is rounded when playing its key (Figure 21). Sometimes it helps if the teacher holds their own pinkie in proper posture somewhere near the keyboard so that the child notices this in their peripheral vision and unconsciously crooks their own finger. At advanced levels the pinkie's posture may vary, depending on the requirements of the piece.

Figure 21

50   #43: Here, Chord I appears as a melodic sequence. The notes should still be referred to by the color names the child now knows.

Instead of "Teddy" other names could be used so the child will practice the melody without perceiving that they have played it before. When using a name for this song that has more than two syllables ("Jen-ni-fer, where are you?"), blue can be played twice at the beginning, or a red can be added before the blue. After one or two lessons the child may be able to play this melody from memory.

It is sometimes helpful if the teacher or parents sing the lyrics, because playing and singing at the same time may not be easy for the child.

52-55   #44-45: Now the child is able to play two simple songs. Again, the teacher or parents may sing the words while the child plays.

The rhythmic notation, of quarter notes and half notes, is deliberately omitted from both of these songs. Because the child can easily recognize the melody, they will be able to play in approximately the correct rhythm. The note types will be introduced later. Here the child is reading and playing many different notes in sequence. The teacher and parents should continue to point at the notes as they are played, not only for this piece but for all subsequent pieces. After about 10-12 months, children will usually be able to practice the pieces without having the notes pointed at; they may even ask the teacher or parent to stop pointing. This does not mean that the teacher should stop and never point at notes again; there are children who will benefit from pointing even at advanced stages. As a general principle, no helpful technique should be completely abandoned.

Sometimes children reject the note-pointing even though it is clearly necessary. If this happens, you can use stuffed animals to point at the notes. When a stuffed animal asks to point, a child rarely refuses.

The posture of the pinkie finger needs special attention in both songs. The bass hand, which is not needed, should be placed motionless on the left thigh. The child should never place their left hand on the chair, because this will allow bad habits of body posture to develop.

The notes are printed on these pages in a smaller size than before, but the child should easily be able to accept them. If the child has trouble seeing these notes, they may need an eye exam. If the smaller notes can be easily read, the child should repeat all the previous pieces in their practice sessions and bring that practice to bear on #44 and 45.

56-60   #46-55: All five sounds have now been introduced for each hand. These pieces contain different note combinations using three, four, or five sounds.

62-64   #56-61: Here the child plays notes which have another note between them. The child has already played some of these "third intervals," in the melody from #44. Although it would have been logical to practice these intervals separately before playing them in a melody, children are normally eager to play a melody.

The child should be allowed to repeat the third interval for as long as they want. This promotes proper technique. The teacher can accompany the child's interval with a simple melody or improvisation, but the accompaniment should never overshadow the child's playing.

65-66   #62-65: These are notes with two other notes between them, or "fourth intervals."

B-flat appears for the first time in #64. The teacher shows the child the associated black key and explains that this key is named "B-flat." If the child doesn't like this name, they may invent another. For example, one child called the note "Spider" for a long time. The teacher can accommodate the child's suggestion by creatively using both names— sometimes "B-flat" and sometimes "Spider."

67   #66-68: This page prepares us for the half note. From this page on, for each half note, the child will stomp their foot on its second beat. The child should first learn to stomp with only one leg; otherwise, their seating stability and performance posture becomes seriously impaired. The child may choose which leg to stomp.

The new sign could be introduced with a question: "What is this new symbol?" The teacher may want to explain that this is a secret sign, that only the child and teacher understand. This can prompt the child to be especially interested in it. The teacher shares the secret, explaining that this sign is a "Stomper" and that, at each mark, the child must stomp loudly on the stool. The child is often so amused by the stomping that they will practice stomping without paying any attention to the printed page. In these first stomping exercises, the teacher should try to guide any wild and uneven stomping into a steady rhythm. This can be accomplished more quickly if the child imagines that the stomping is for some amusing purpose; for example, the child can pretend to pump up an air mattress with a foot pedal.

If the child is unable to stomp in rhythm or stomps only with difficulty, the teacher can try replacing the Stomper with a click of the tongue or lips. This method has proven effective with children who have coordination difficulties.

If, with full parental support and no serious mistakes from the teacher, the child still has difficulty with color/finger or finger/key coordination, this may reveal a problem with the child's normal development. The parents should at that point seek professional advice. For the child's further development, existing interference should be assessed and treated before entering school.

After these introductory strategies, the child is able to attempt #66-68 with the correct Stompers. Practicing #66-68 each day at home serves as preparation for the pages of the next lesson.

68-77 #69-88: A half note is now added to the simple scale that has already been practiced. It is at the end of each practice line. The child should be told that the Stomper has the same timing as the preceding quarter notes.

Starting with #69, the half and quarter notes look different from each other. The half notes have a small hole in the middle, and they are always followed by a Stomper sign. The notes are now all drawn with stems; the child may or may not notice this change. At this stage, it's not important to learn the terms "quarter note" and "half note"; it's only important to play them correctly. The child will learn the notes' names later.

When playing the half note, the child must learn that the finger leaves the key only after the stomping; the teacher may gently hold their finger on the key along with the child, so that the child does not remove their finger too early.

78-82 #89-98: Each of these pieces has both a step (such as C-D) and a leap (such as D-F). Repeated practice of these combinations will improve elementary piano skills. If necessary, the teacher may draw other notes in this same configuration for the child to play.

83-84 #99-102: Here are triads to be played. These three-note combinations are in the same rhythm as the previous ones, but they use only third intervals.

86-89 #103-106: These pieces are all two measures long— this is longer than the previous pieces— and each ends with a half-note, which requires a Stomper. The Stomper at the end of each piece must be "played" in time with the notes. Sometimes, the teacher must make large rhythmic movements along with the child's playing to encourage the child to play rhythmically.

90-91	#107: This is the first time the child plays with both hands alternately. When a hand is not being used, it should rest at the edge of the keys or at least near the keyboard. In changing measures, the child needs to understand that they can play legato even when moving from one hand to another. This happens with the D (right) to C (left) between measures 1-2 and 3-4, and B (left) to C (right) between measures 2-3. Both of these combinations can be practiced by themselves, separate from #107.
92-93	#108: This piece expands the sound area to three fingers on each hand. Again the end of measure 2 has a D-C which should be played legato. Measure 5 is harder to play legato, because in this measure the right hand unexpectedly plays the D, and the change between hands is abrupt. If the child plays the third note in measure 5 (which is a C) with their right hand, then they must change back to the left hand for the B. Using the right hand to play C is acceptable, even though it is not marked that way in the piece. Because children of this age should not be corrected, or corrected only with great care, the teacher should express acceptance of this usage before suggesting an alternative.

In the last measure, the same note is repeated. Attentive children will recognize that this is the same note played with two different hands.

It is extremely important that the child plays this piece "without holes" in a fluid, legato motion.

94-95	#109: For the first time, two successive half notes with different pitch sounds appear. The piece is also ended with a whole note which requires three Stompers. With the whole note it is advisable, at least at first, to touch the child's finger gently until the key is to be released. The child must concentrate on two things:

1. They must stomp three times.

2. While stomping, their finger continues to press the key.

96-98	#110: This is the first time that the child repeats a single sound on the same hand. The child may have already learned this song as a finger game. If so, the child may play one verse of the song on the piano, after which the teacher plays and sings the verse while the child plays the familiar finger game. All three verses can be approached this way.
99	#111: For the first time, the treble and bass hands play simultaneously, in parallel movement. At the conclusion of the piece, both thumbs press the middle C together. There is normally

sufficient space on the key for the two small thumbs of a child. Notice there is only one Stomper at the end; the child should stomp with only one foot.

100-102   #112: Finding the blue (G) at the end of the second measure is not easy. If the child has trouble, the note may be highlighted by a sticker on the page, directly over or under the note (a blue sticker, if possible), but the child should be informed that the bass hand may not be lifted too far from the keys. If the sound repetitions at the ends of measure 4 or the final measure are too hard to do with both hands, the child may use the treble hand by itself.

103   #113: In the final measure a note with exactly two Stompers appears for the first time. The child must be alerted to the change in the third measure; otherwise they may repeat the first measure. The use of the three-beat measure is also new. This should not be stated, but shown through rhythmic presentation of the notes.

104-105   #114: Now that the child has practiced the three-beat measure, this piece explores the three-beat measure.

106-108   #115: In the "Raindrop Song", which returns to four-beat time, the bass hand plays more notes than the treble hand. The treble hand must be kept ready, however; the child may not place their hand on their thigh, on the chair, or behind their back.

109-111   #116: In measures 4, 5, and 6, pay attention to the bass hand's pinkie finger to ensure good form.

Volume Two

Pages

4-5   #117-118: Here the child learns the repeat sign. To make the child curious, the teacher can let them notice the new sign for themselves, then explain "this is the 'repeat sign.'" In a child's words this may become the "do-again" sign, or even "I play the song again." What the sign is called doesn't matter. What the child *must* come to understand is that measure 1 follows measure 2 *without any pause*.

It is good technical training for a child to play the two-measure pieces continuously. Unlike adults, children do not get easily bored by repetitive activity. Rather, a constant repetition becomes a kind of game. Just think of how much a child enjoys building something with blocks, knocking it down, and rebuilding it.

6-7   #119-120: In these two pieces, the rhythm is reversed.

8-15	**#121-122:** Both of these songs reappear in Volume Three, on pages 20-23, although the notes' size is larger here. A smaller size is not suitable for the current level. The teacher must turn the page smoothly from 9 to 10, so that the child's rhythm is not hindered. It often helps the child if a colored yellow dot is stuck to page 9, after the last measure, in the D position. This prepares them for the first sound on the next page.
	#122 combines a number of tasks which have been previously practiced: a half note at the beginning of a measure, sound repetitions, notes with two Stompers, and the repeat sign. Therefore, this piece requires extra concentration and must be played at a slow speed. Because of the repetition, this piece is also longer than all the earlier ones. For these reasons, this piece can be too daunting for some children, in which case it may be skipped and returned to later, possibly in conjunction with **#204** (in Volume Three).
16-19	**#123:** Here the teacher must monitor the rhythm of the whole notes in measures 2, 4, 10, and 12, making sure that the child does not delay the measures after each whole note.
20-23	**#124:** This is the first song that features a repetition with a different end measure. Because children of this age often don't read numbers, the measures are marked with one or two hearts. Other symbols or stickers can be drawn or placed over the corresponding measures, if the child wishes. In measure 5, the teacher should make sure that the three repetitions of A are played in the proper meter; children are often biased toward accelerating the Stompers' tempo.
24-27	**#125-126:** In these long practices for the bass and treble hands, the teacher has to point at the sounds slightly in advance, so that the child can play without stopping. Next to rhythmic playing, good finger posture is most important, especially for the pinkie finger. This piece should not be played too quickly. Often, when this piece is described as a long "note snake," the child plays it more easily.
28-29	**#127-128:** In this sequence the child's attention must be drawn to the transition between measures 3 and 4, because the movement direction suddenly changes.
30-31	**#129-130:** Similar to the preceding practice, the difficulty here is in the transition between measures 4 and 5. In measures 5 and 6 the pinkie finger's posture must be given special attention.
32-45	These pieces contain a series of practices for each hand. Numbers 132, 134, 136, 139, 140, and 142 are derived from "Preschool Piano

Playing" by Ferdinand Beyer. Numbers 131, 133, 135, and 141 are mirror images of the Beyer exercises. A corresponding practice series follows in #149-168.

The question arises, why do we use so many practice pieces from 19th-century piano training? For several reasons, which we want to clarify in a short digression.

The piano training of Ferdinand Beyer emerged at a time when the major-minor system was established as the base component of musical thinking and perceiving. From this understanding Beyer wrote a large number of pieces for children to practice, pieces which fulfill two goals: they reinforce a certain harmonic feeling of major or minor, and they develop a child's piano technique.

At the end of the 19th and the beginning of the 20th century, there were several piano training methods of this type, although Beyer's can be regarded as the most successful. Beyer understood the necessity of composing exercises for piano technique in combination with musical language, and children enthusiastically enjoy his work.

In the 20th century the major-minor system was expanded for composition, and gradually replaced by other systems. This naturally affected children's musical training; different methods have been tried since then, with varying levels of success. The instructional curriculum *We Hear and Play* is the result of our many years of teaching children. To succeed most fully in their musicianship, children must develop a home-base understanding of sound. Absolute pitch, and an understanding of harmony, develops only if a child hears intensively the principal components of a major key. Combined with piano instruction, the decision to use C-major was obvious. To solidify their playing technique, a child should hear and play all C-major sounds from the very start of their training (see page 24). The selection of notes for practice material was a result of logical study; nonetheless, we wished to take into account childlike preferences. Therefore, we integrated practices from Beyer's piano training, sometimes in transposed, reversed, or altered form.

Regrettably, Beyer's work has been neglected. The criticism of piano training from his era mostly lumps together the various methods of the time as though they came from a single theory of training, without seriously evaluating the contents of individual curricula. Because of this, the ordinary, unremarkable piano training of the 19th century is usually not distinguished from the outstanding, pedagogically significant work that Beyer produced. In using Beyer's work we have integrated into our method a proven, traditional system of musical training.

#131-132: After practicing this piece a number of times, a child usually can play it from memory, together with the teacher's accompaniment. As has been repeatedly emphasized, the accompaniment should unobtrusively support the child's playing.

#133-134: A child usually plays the first note of a repeated sound with a short stroke, almost staccato. At this age level, this is not a problem.

#135-136: Measures 4 and 8 must be thought of as continuations of the quarter-note rhythm, with the Stompers in proper meter. Measure 5 must follow measure 4 without a pause or break.

#137-138: For the notes that directly precede or follow B-flat, the white keys must be pressed further back on the keyboard. The entire hand should move slightly forward, toward the black keys, before returning to its original position.

#139-140: In these practices, the child begins to gain a feeling for classic musical patterns. The use of broken triads encourages the children toward typical inventions.

#141-142: The Stomper must be carried out precisely in time. Therefore, these pieces should not be played at too fast a tempo.

46-51   #143-144: If possible, the child should play all the verses. The teacher or parents can sing along.

52-54   #145. In playing measures 2 and 4, which each have a B-flat, follow the same directions as for #137-138.

55-57   #146: The change between hands will gradually become less difficult. The idle hand should remain in position near the keys.

58-61   #147-148: Switching hands must now occur without breaks or pauses. The sounds B-flat and F-sharp should be fully integrated into the ear training.

62-65   #149-152: The steady rhythm of pieces #149 and #150 is altered in measure 7. This often causes pauses. The teacher can help prevent this through an active, rhythmic pointing at the notes. #151 and #152 are variations of #149 and #150.

66-81   #153-168: Children may find these practices entertaining, and the practices are important for further artistic progress, melodic comprehension, and playing technique. If, at a later level, a child is able to play more difficult pieces, it is still highly recommended to return to these practices again and again to reinforce what has been learned. Through the directed playing of these pieces, which have roughly the same degree of difficulty, the child gradually attains a feeling for the music.

It is our intention that these pieces should be easy for children and played more or less effortlessly. Only then will a child be pleased with their own piano playing. If they can only play the pieces with great effort, they will lose the desire to play. This will happen especially if the preceding pieces were played incompletely, or infrequently; it can happen if absolute pitch is not developed in conjunction with the pieces. Hearing development and advancing piano skills are tightly connected.

If, in spite of good instruction, a child is unable to play these pieces fluently, other factors may be responsible, like motor awkwardness or perceptual problems. In such cases the teacher should let the child repeat old pieces out of Volumes One and Two to consolidate the feeling for fluent piano playing.

In #165 and #166 there appears, for the first time, a quarter rest. It should be explained here only if the child asks; otherwise it can be taken for granted. If the rest is explained at this point, it will be less important to emphasize it when playing "The Goose" (#177).

82-85   #169-171: From #169 onward, the size of the notes is once again reduced. Because this means an adjustment for the child, the difficulty of these pieces is deliberately decreased. Like in other songs, the child should play all the verses while the teacher or parents sing.

86-90   #172-175: The teacher's task is to develop with the child a feeling for playing piano as though the child were "singing" through the instrument.

91   #176: This piece has already been played, as #140, but with larger notes. An attentive child will see this right away and should be praised for noticing.

92-93   #177: The quarter rest, which appeared for the first time in #165 and #166, shows up three times in this song. The child must gradually learn that the finger leaves the key during the rest but that the hand must not leave the keyboard, and that the measure after the rest must begin on time. The teacher may help the child by carefully leading the corresponding finger to the next correct key.

94-98   #178-180: Through adept guidance from the teacher, the child can be helped to play these songs expressively. If the parent who is present at the instruction "falls asleep" when the piece is played smoothly, the child is often highly motivated to play well; they are greatly amused at being able to make their parents fall asleep and wake up again. With attention to technique (no errors, good posture) the child's concentration can be increased. If the child enjoys this kind of response to their playing, the strategy can be repeated with other pieces.

In #180 the sustaining tie is used for the first time. The child should be informed that the G (blue) in the final measure is not played again but is counted in addition to the preceding note. To make this point easier to understand, a little Stomper sign appears underneath the last note.

99-104   #181-186: These pieces look easy to an adult, but children need to concentrate when playing them. If the teacher doesn't point, the number of notes the child plays rarely matches the number of notes on the page. In #184 the transition from measure 4 to 5 should get special attention; in the middle of the 4th measure, the teacher can caution the child to be ready for the change. In #185 the child must figure out which hand plays red or blue.

105   #187: This simple song, similar to #169, is suitable for playing from memory.

106-107   #188: In this song, many tones are repeated. The teacher should continue to point at the notes, so that the child maintains tempo and rhythm and does not lose their place in the melody.

108-109   #189: Some children may find it difficult to tell whether they should play the low or high blue note at the beginning of each line (measures 5, 9, and 13). Each of these blue notes is preceded by a Stomper; while the child is stomping, the teacher should touch the child's correct finger, right before the blue note is to be played.

110-111   #190: In "Floating", the change of hands shouldn't disrupt the movement of the melody. The melody should be played with a flowing motion, like a bird gliding through the air. When the child learns to play this piece more confidently, the tempo may be increased.

Volume Three

Pages

3-4   #191: After the child plays this song, it is a good idea to revisit some earlier pieces (#178-180 are recommended).

6-7	#192-193: In both pieces, all transitions should be played smoothly. It is good practicing technique if the child first plays the treble hand and the teacher the bass, and then they switch places. To avoid pauses, a slower speed is recommended.
8	#194: This fun little song serves as relaxation after two difficult pieces. The child may recognize the melody as identical to "Yankee Doodle Dandy."
9-15	#195-197: In #195 both thumbs press middle C (red) simultaneously. This should not be a problem for little fingers. In #196 and #197, the child may play only the treble hand while the teacher plays the bass hand. If the child plays these pieces with both hands together, the teacher should help the child play the bass hand. The child gets the feel for correctly playing the left-hand sound repetition. After practicing repeatedly in this manner, they can play the piece without the teacher's help.
16-18	#198-200: Here, also, these three pieces can be practiced first with the child playing treble and the teacher playing bass, and then switching so that the child plays bass and the teacher treble. In all three pieces, the quarter notes carry the rhythm, so that Stomper signs are only necessary in the last measure. If the child practices with only one hand, it's a good idea to pencil in Stomper signs where they belong. Once the child is able to play the piece with both hands, these signs can be erased.
19	#201-202: Each of these pieces is for the left or right hand to play separately and alone. Each piece should be played consecutively for as long as possible. It's often motivating to hold an endurance contest between child and teacher. The teacher can play along with the child, softly, in a higher octave or on a different piano. The one who plays the longest wins. While playing, the teacher may tell the child that they can't go on much longer, which will encourage the child to continue a little further. The teacher can control the playing tempo and sometimes may want to carefully increase the speed.
20-23	#203-204: The child knows these pieces already from where they were printed with larger notes in #121 and #122.
24-25	#205: This piece should be played so that it gradually becomes fluid. The repetitions can also be played quasi-staccato. Basically, the child may have freedom in articulating the notes.

26-27	#206-207: These longer practices are rhythmic and played at constant volume. The quarter rest in the middle of the etude should be noted and carried out cleanly.
28-29	#208-209: These pieces offer practices for the quarter rest in both 4/4 and 3/4 time. Inventive children may discover that, where there is a rest, they can click their tongue or say one of their favorite words. The teacher might also do something surprising or funny during each rest.
30-31	#210: This piece has many quarter rests which need to be timed correctly. When first playing this piece slowly, the child should play the piano with a singing quality to the tone.
32-35	#211-212: Here the same song is played in two different keys, to begin developing a feeling for transposition. The tempo must not be changed between measures 8 and 9.
36-37	#213: In addition to the accurate timing of the rests, the teacher must ensure that the sound repetitions do not fall out of rhythm in measures 5-8.
38-39	#214: The piece should first be played slowly. The student may then increase the tempo provided that the playing quality does not suffer. Children who are less skilled or have coordination difficulties should try this piece later in their training.
40-41	#215: The first time through, this melody should be played without the bass-hand accompaniment. Even so, the child will notice that, in the next-to-last measure, a note from the melody is played with the bass hand. When playing with both hands, special attention must be given to the rests in the bass line. It sometimes helps if the teacher draws a circle around the rests, using the child's favorite color, so that they may be more obvious.
42-43	#216-217: These two pieces practice eighth-note rhythms. Their rhythms are essentially the same as each other, although the direction of movement is reversed.
44-45	#218-220: After the previous practices, the child can play these pieces somewhat effortlessly. In #219 and #220 the beginning line should be repeated consecutively with each hand.
46-47	#221-222: At the end of #221 the major third is split between hands. In #222 this happens repeatedly. To accomplish this in proper rhythm, both hands should stay near the keyboard.

48-49	#223-224: As always, the teacher's accompaniment should be discreet.
50-51	#225-226: In #225 the eighth notes appear in the same rhythm as before. However, in #226 the eighth note always occurs on the third beat. With the downbeat and the following eighth notes, the teacher could create an exercise like an improvisation beginning from different tones. The teacher may first play the rhythmic motif, and then the child answers by playing the same motif with other tones.
52-53	#227: In the second part of this song, the eighth-note usage is expanded. Therefore it should be played slowly at first. The rests and half notes should be played correctly in addition to the eighth notes.
54	#228 A-B: The alternation between both hands here is not new, but it is presented here in combinations of eighth and quarter notes. The practice goal is to gain a feeling for switching hands and also for the rhythmic changes between eighth and quarter notes.
	#228 C-F: The most important task here is to attack the upper area of the key for the white keys adjacent to the F#. In #228C the third finger presses near the tip of the black key; the pinkie presses between F# and G#. This also applies to the fourth finger in practices D, E, and F.
55	#229: The melody of the minuets from Bach's "Notenbüchlein Für Anna Magdalena" is divided here between both hands. Because of the previous practices, the child can master this, and will also manage the rhythmic problems of the pieces that follow. The child will gradually play in a more expressive manner and should therefore be given pieces of differing moods. Describing them as "cheerful" or "sad" can encourage this understanding. Sometimes it is helpful to invent a story or lyrics to motivate the child.
56-59	#230: A child who has been developing their absolute pitch will be able to play this song quickly from memory. They may sometimes begin playing the melody on a different starting note, however, and continue playing in a different key signature. This is acceptable and should be supported.
	#231: So that the fourth finger of the treble hand can play F-sharp, the adjoining fingers must press further back on the white keys, and the piece should be played at a slower tempo.
	#232: The child knows this first measure, but they know it with a dotted rhythm. If they wish to play it that way, the rhythm can be

altered by adding a dot to the one note and an eighth-flag to the other's stem. During the half rest in measure 4, the teacher can sing a word like "Pau-se" softly in rhythm on the third and fourth beats.

60-61 #233-234: With both pieces, the eighth-note rhythm in the fourth measure is practiced.

62 #235: Measures 3 and 7 are more complicated and therefore require greater concentration. It is difficult to motivate children to practice a single measure or section. Therefore, these places require the teacher to draw increased attention to the notes by adept gestures.

63 #236: The child has already experienced the change of one time signature to another. This can be done more deliberately in #235 and #236, because both songs begin in different time signatures with similar melodies. At this stage, the child will be able to count the repeated tones in the first measure.

64 #237: The preceding piece used the treble hand almost exclusively; in #237, the bass hand predominates.

65 #238: As was recommended for #229, this piece should be played with a certain character. In measure 6, after the eighth notes have ended, the teacher can support the new movement by pointing at the notes in the correct rhythm.

66-67 #239: The purpose of this piece is to become familiar with all the different note values.

68-70 #240-242: These three songs begin with a pickup measure of two eighth notes. In #240 the pickup measure is a single sound repetition. In the transition between measures 4 and 5, the treble hand must be able to reach the high octave. Because this occurs while changing from the first to second line on the page, it's helpful to draw a blue mark at the end of the first line, to remind the child that this note is to be played next. In #241, the student must pay special attention to the pinkie finger in the next-to-last measure.

71 #243: In measures 5 and 6, the teacher must help in the execution of the quarter rest. The teacher can clap, for example, or find another way to fill the empty space.

72 #244-245: As in #124 from Volume Two, the changed repeat measure is represented by one or two hearts. In the following polka, #245, the hearts are replaced with the numbers 1 and 2. In this way the child learns the meaning without theoretical explanations.

73   **#246:** The child should play all repetitions in this piece. Children often avoid this, preferring to skip repetitions.

74   **#247:** The direction *"DC al Fine"* is new here and must be explained. The second ending should be played with the capo. The teacher's pointing at the notes while the child is playing will make it easier to understand.

75   **#248:** After this song is played, the E-flat should be incorporated into the daily hearing exercises. By this time the child should have good development in their absolute hearing of the C-major sounds.

76-77   **#249:** This piece must be played in a precise, medium tempo. In measure 5, the second eighth note should be played quickly because of the subsequent sound repetition.

78-79   **#250:** In measure 4, no pause should occur in the transition of the treble hand to the bass hand. The same instruction applies to all of page 79. The child should not remove their hands from the keyboard. Adept children can play this piece at a relatively fast tempo before too long; they enjoy the fast movement.

80-82   **#251:** This lengthy piece requires careful attention throughout. Technical attention is needed for the sound repetition in measure 7, to make sure of the correct finger position near the black keys, and to ensure the rhythmic and speedy execution of the eighth notes.

83   **#252:** In measures 5 and 7, after the first quarter note, make sure of the timely release of the key in either the bass or treble hand.

85-86   **#253:** The tempo should not be too fast, so that the variety of note values can be played in the desired rhythm. The sound repetition in the first measure is to be carried out as noted, with changing hands.

86-87   **#254:** The eighth notes in measures 3, 4, and 7 may be practiced in isolation. It's possible to form a new, shorter practice piece from these eighth notes alone.

88-89   **#255:** The quiet, steady speed of this piece helps the child perceive the minor character of the melody. As has been mentioned repeatedly, the teacher's accompaniment should be discreet.

90   **#256:** Because of the many eighth notes, the tempo must not be too fast. The quarter rests must be clear and exact. In measures 3 and 4, when playing the octave spread between low G and middle G, there must be no delay. This means that the treble hand should not leave the keys.

91 #257: The printed verses encourage the child to play the song multiple times.

92-93 #258: At the beginning, the pinkie finger of the treble hand must attack further up on the key, in the area of the black keys, so that the fourth finger is prepared to play the F-sharp. To emphasize the character of the march, the first note of each measure can be accented.

94-95 #259: The ratio of the note values in measures 1 and 2, as well the repetitions of both measures, must conform to each other. There must be no delay between the final two eighth notes of the first measure. For the child to grasp the rhythm of the piece, the teacher can play the minuet continually while the child dances with the parents.

96-97 #260: The teacher must pay close attention to the many sound repetitions and their exact rhythmic execution. The children may want to do additional verses with other animals.

98-99 #261: This is the first time a dotted quarter note is used, with a smaller Stomper sign. The teacher explains to the child that the faster eighth note should be played directly after this smaller, possibly softer Stomper. The teacher may quietly play or sing the song along with the child, either in a higher octave or on a second piano.

100-101 #262: For the child to better feel the rhythm, especially the continuous beat, the teacher can play the song while the child runs at the speed of the quarter notes. These notes should have a somewhat ponderous character.

102-103 #263-264: The bass hand takes on the function of the small Stompers from the preceding songs. First the child should play with the bass hand only. The second time, the teacher plays the treble hand while the child plays bass. The third time, the teacher plays bass while the child plays treble.

104-109 #265-267: These three songs also help reinforce dotted-note rhythms.

110-111 #268 A-F: For the first time the playing area is expanded to further octaves in both directions. By now, all the white keys of the piano should be marked with corresponding colored dots (see also page 31).

Practices A and B, when repeated, begin to seem like a dance, and the teacher may play a waltz along with the child. Practices C-F are to be carried out with stricter rhythm; therefore, the child should first play them without the teacher's accompaniment.

112 #269: In the octave spread the hand should be able to reach far enough to straddle both keys. It is good practice to let the child repeatedly stretch and relax their hand before attempting these pieces. This can be done either at the keyboard or away from it.

113-115 #270-273: In #270 the octaves are practiced differently. In A and B, the second and fourth note are most naturally played staccato; in C, the octave shift may be best accomplished by an elastic arm movement.

In #271 and #272 the treble and bass hands cross into the other staff for the first time. For this the child's sitting position may have to change. The seat may have to be moved further away from the keyboard, so that the child may be able to attempt larger arm movements.

116 #274-275: The treble hand plays two practices in its new place. When discovering these sounds for the first time, the child may need the teacher's help, because they may not be able to distinguish the octave heights of the notes.

From #274 onward, a time signature appears in all pieces. The child will notice this gradually and unconsciously. Not all children are able to read numbers at this age; therefore, the teacher need not explain the theoretical meaning of the time signature. It's better to wait until the child gains the reasoning power to understand it.

117-118 #276-277: These practices are for the treble hand only. The teacher's accompaniment must remain in the background.

119-125 #278-280: Although the melody of these pieces are in the new octaves, the bass hand remains in its original octave.

For #278 and the exercises that follow, we recommend that the teacher and child play together, alternating who plays which hand.

In #280 the fourth and fifth fingers of the treble hand are emphasized.

On page 125 the use of F-sharp and F (orange) within the same measure is interesting for the child but requires increased concentration.

126 #281: Here the sound repetitions in the bass hand must be played carefully. The treble hand should be legato, if possible. Delays and breaks between measures should be avoided. In measure 8, the bass hand must be extended over an octave for the first time in a musical piece, although the extension itself was practiced in #269.

127	#282-283: These practices correspond to #276-277, but they are to be played with the bass hand.
128-129	#284: For the first time both hands play together in their new octaves. In the transition between pages 128 and 129, the child must increase their concentration to avoid problems while changing hands. In conjunction with this piece, the child can return to #276 and #277 and play the same melody with the bass hand. After that, both hands can play the melody in unison, with the bass hand on high C and the treble hand on the next highest C. Adults may see a contradiction in calling the left hand "bass hand" when it is playing treble keys. The child will not be confused by this, and it will have no negative effects on their further musical development.
130-131	#285: This piece should be first attempted at a slow tempo, because of the changing of the hands.
132-136	#286-289: These pieces should be played at a tempo which allows them to be sonorous and expressive. In #289 the meaning of "Da Capo" must again be explained.

Advanced Training

Expanding the Sound Area

Black Keys

Black keys must be incorporated into the ear training as soon as they appear in *We Hear and Play*. The first two are B-flat and F-sharp. With the black keys, the note names are used right away; in the ball game, the child should choose both grey *and* purple for B-flat, and orange *and* blue for F-sharp.

The black key sounds become familiar through hearing and guessing. With the black keys, it is useful to let the child play back the notes they hear; otherwise, their similar names can easily lead to verbal confusion. C-sharp, E-flat, and A-flat should be slowly incorporated; even if the child easily recognizes all other sounds of the entire keyboard, these three tones will still take more time. They will eventually be included in the child's perception of absolute pitch, provided that the listening exercises are continued regularly.

Keyboard Dots

At the start of instruction, only the nine white keys between low F and middle G should be marked with colored dots. Once the child hears these sounds absolutely, the remaining white keys can be dotted. This is good for technical reasons, and eventually it becomes necessary (starting with Volume 3, #268). However, the game area should not be expanded until the child has a firm grasp of the home octave.

New Octaves

After 1½ years of training, if the child can confidently recognize all white keys in the home octave as well as B-flat and F-sharp, the sound area can be carefully expanded. The teacher plays middle C followed by high C and asks the child about the color. Sometimes a child guesses that high C is also red, but the most common answer is "blue." If the child answers "blue," the teacher tells the child to listen again carefully, and repeats middle C followed by high C. If the child still doesn't recognize the C, the teacher can explain that this sound is also red, but a *lighter* red. The teacher may continue with "dark" red (low C). Both new sounds should then be incorporated into the daily practices until they are well-recognized.

The entire range of sound is thus gradually opened. This happens easily with attentive and well-guided children. By this time the child should also be playing low C through G with their left hand and middle C through G with their right hand. At this stage of hearing a teacher may also ask a child to sing a specific tone without the aid of the piano.

Ongoing Development

The child's ear will gradually learn all the different piano sounds. Our experience has shown that very low sounds are more difficult to recognize than very high sounds. After becoming familiar with the piano's sound, the child will begin recognizing sounds from other sources and will learn to determine the octave height of pitches. Initially, a child's absolute pitch ability may be tied to the piano they are learning with, and he or she will make more hearing mistakes with an unfamiliar piano. This is normal, and disappears with increasing hearing ability. Direct association of sound and color can sometimes occur; a child may hear the "grey" of a cow bell or knock his head against the wall and hear "orange."

Ear training instruction should be continued until the child is at least 12 years old. Otherwise, their developed absolute pitch may disappear. Regular piano tuning is absolutely necessary.

Interfering Factors

- Prolonged exposure to loud music, often through radio and television

- Constantly changing the practice instrument

- Poorly maintained or out-of-tune practice or teaching instruments

- Lengthy interruptions of regular practice (such as frequent vacations)

- Always using different keys when singing children's songs at home

- Methodological mistakes by the teacher and parents.

Introducing Traditional Notation

Readers may wonder, "Why not work with traditional black and white notes immediately instead of colored notes?" Any educator who works with little children, however, will see that doing so is impractical.

Our musical training begins at 3-4½, at which age children can't yet process the multilevel schemes of spatial construction required by traditional notation. To be able to read notes in this system, a child needs to distinguish between the five lines and measure all the intervals visually. This is not possible at such a young age. Persistent attempts to teach this usually cause frustration and denial. By using colors, we avoid this problem and focus instead on developing the child's inherent musical abilities.

This process is similar to learning one's native language, which begins much earlier than any musical instruction. A child can construct complicated sentences, and express profound thoughts, long before they can read or write. Only after the native tongue is well understood does a child learn to read and write. When we transfer this process to musical education, it is clear that a child should be able to identify tones, chords, and melodies by ear, and be able to play them, before learning to read traditional notation.

Colored notes make this possible. In the *We Hear and Play* system, colored notes help a child to develop absolute pitch, which then enables the child to freely sing and play the sounds that they hear and read. Traditional notation is only meaningful to a child who has achieved this level of understanding.

Colored notes are essential because they allow a child to hear and play even in early childhood. They teach the child to play piano at an age when traditional notation is still too abstract to understand. Furthermore, colored notes provide an ideal foundation for when a child does learn black notes in later training. This is why *We Hear and Play* uses colored notes, and it is also why we use color names instead of letter names or solfege syllables.

Colored notes allow the gradual introduction of traditional (black and white) notation. For this systematic introduction, the three volumes of *We Hear and Play* should be used and returned to. Traditional notes and their letter names are introduced together no earlier than age 5 (and preferably later).

Traditional notation must be taught thoroughly and with correct methodology. The process takes about two years, during which time the child should continue to use colored notes. After completing *We Hear and Play* Volume Three, ordinary piano music can be colored for a child's continued instruction (see page 67).

Although it seems like 3- to 5-year-old children can learn note reading, what appears to be note reading is most likely some other process. When a small child sits in front of a page of black notes, they appear to be playing the music on that page, but they are not really reading the notes. Rather, the sounds and movement are flowing from memory.

It is possible for somewhat older children (5-6 years old) to read traditional notes; however, their capacity for free musical expression is limited because so much of their effort must be applied to reading the notes. Unfortunately, note literacy is rarely taught to children, and any child who does not learn it will be unable to fully realize their musical ability. One can see this in children age 10 and above who can read notes, but can only do so slowly and with great effort. In such cases note reading becomes an intolerable hindrance, and the child's frustration at their inability to succeed creates mental barriers. Each new attempt at playing feels like a terrible effort. Sometimes students continue to study music, but each piece takes so long to learn they become intensely dissatisfied. Other children may give up completely. In any case, it is only through success and advancement that a child can become enthusiastic about their piano playing.

Being trained to read the notes is vital. In normal schooling, children begin learning their native language immediately, with a high priority placed on literacy. They study language for several hours every week. They are taught both to read and to express themselves in written language. Although the children can already speak their native language, it is reintroduced to them in a new form so that they gain mastery of it. They begin by reading simple sentences, either silently or out loud with other children. Over and over they write letters and words, both in school and at home. A child who finishes grade school and still can't read a newspaper is considered a failure.

It seems obvious that a child should be able to read and write their native language. But rarely is a similar need recognized in musical training. Instruction normally focuses on tasks other than literacy. Yet even if a child's weekly music lesson were dedicated entirely to note-reading, we can see— by comparison to the amount of time and energy devoted to learning one's language— that this is not nearly enough.

To be musically literate, the child must learn three permanent skills:

1. They must be able to decode and read the notes.

2. The notes, when read, must evoke the appropriate sounds in the child's mind.

3. The child must be able to immediately create the sounds thus read (and mentally heard) on their chosen instrument.

Because musical instruction receives so much less time than language training, the best way to achieve these goals is, over several years, to dedicate a segment of the weekly lesson exclusively to note reading.

Children who learn to read notes must be able to create music. They must *know* the tones they are producing; only then can black and white notes be meaningful. Our solution is to introduce a child to the world of piano, music, and tones by singing and playing colored notes; this is the main reason for using colored notes.

Children who begin *We Hear and Play* at age 3 or 4, and play for two years using colored notes, will gain absolute pitch and learn essential hearing skills.

The correct time to introduce traditional notation is, of course, dependent on a child's development. In most cases it is meaningful only after some schooling.

Introductory Phase

To learn traditional notation, the child returns to *We Hear and Play* Volume One, approximately two years after opening that book for the first time.

This introduction must not occur too early, or the teacher's earlier work is destroyed. Eager parents often think of colored notes as something to get past quickly. They want their child to start reading black notes as soon as possible so they suggest that colored notes are incorrect or abnormal. However, for an effective introduction to traditional notes, training with colored notes is absolutely necessary. Without thorough preparation, attempting to learn traditional notation is not just difficult, but meaningless.

The first step is learning the note names. Still using the colored notes and not yet referring to the staff lines, the teacher informs the child of the note names B, D, A, and E; then C, and finally F and G. The child learns that each note, which before has been called (for example) "purple," can now be called "B" as in "ball." This new label must be repeated as homework and carried over into the next lesson. Effective homework is indispensable.

It is best if the note names are introduced in the same order as in Volume One. After a few weeks the child will develop a routine for translating colors to note names. All of Volume One should be used for this purpose. The child should see that this introduction is always only a small part of each lesson (about 5 minutes of a 45-minute session).

Usually this can begin at age 6 or 7. The note names may already have been introduced in their school's music curriculum, in which case the *We Hear and Play* instructor reinforces that material.

Once the child has mastered the translation of colors to note names in the C-major scale, the teacher returns to B-flat and F-sharp, in Volume One (#64) and Volume Two (#147 and #148). Even though these two note labels were used from the beginning, the teacher now explains that they too have their own names.

The second step is learning the note lines. Volume One (#1-43) should again be used. The child should learn to count the lines from bottom to top:

————————————	5th line
————————————	4th line
————————————	3rd line
————————————	2nd line
————————————	1st line

Normally this counting is easy for a 5-year-old child. If the child has difficulty, the teacher should defer this step. Once the staff lines have been taught, the child should do homework to reinforce this learning. For example, effective homework can be

1. The child can count the lines, out loud, three times every day.

2. The parent points to a line, and the child names it.

<u>The third step is counting spaces between the lines.</u> Counting spaces is more difficult, for conceptual as well as linguistic reasons. If the child finds the word *space* unfamiliar or confusing, the word *room* can be substituted.

	4th (between) room
	3rd (between) room
	2nd (between) room
	1st (between) room

Homework must reinforce this third task, just as it did first two. After these drills, the child will learn the position of the keys as they correspond to the notes on the page.

<u>The fourth step is learning where the clefs are positioned.</u> To start with, just as at the very beginning, the child is shown only the two musical clefs (Volume One, pages 6 and 7). Now, however, the child learns to draw both of them. To make this more entertaining the child may draw the clefs with exaggerated movements of their finger in the air. The teacher should allow the child to attempt this on their own. The teacher can also put tracing paper over the pages to allow the child to copy the clefs.

The clefs should then be integrated into the staff. This practice requires note paper. We recommend a musical notebook with two pre-printed staves per page, in landscape orientation. The child should be able to

1. Draw both clef symbols accurately enough to be recognized

2. Draw the clefs in their correct positions.

The child may find these suggestions helpful:

1. The bass clef has two dots, which sit in the third and fourth "rooms". The dots can also be described as "under and over" the fourth line.

2. The treble clef begins (or ends) on the second line.

<u>Once these four steps have been taken</u>, the child has this homework:

1. Every day, the child counts the five note lines and draws an entire line of bass clefs. In a notebook that has two staves per page, a page should be filled after two days. After they have drawn the clefs, the child should be encouraged to doodle freely on the other side of the page; this provides emotional release after the intellectual task of repeating clef symbols. The child shows both sides to the teacher at the next lesson.

2. The child repeats #1, but using the treble instead of the bass clef, and they count spaces instead of lines.

3. As a meaningful supplement, the child paints or draws freely using musical symbols such as the clefs. This provides additional emotional release from the intellectual task.

4. After the child can count the lines and spaces with some skill, their next challenge is to mix the lines and spaces. The parent points to any line or space, and the child names it.

Main Phase

In this phase we connect the visual experience to the piano playing, creating the association between the lines, sounds, and keyboard positions. Because the colored notes have always been placed correctly on the staff, many children recognize their positions, although the awareness has been incomplete.

The child first learns the "special" lines: bass F and treble G.

Using #41 the teacher shows how the fourth line runs through both dots of the bass clef. The child follows the line across the page and discovers that there is a note "threaded" on this line, like a bead on a string. This note is now called "F." (If the piano has a cover lock, the child may discover that the F key is in the same position and use the lock for orientation.) The teacher then uses #42 to show that the second line is where the treble clef ends and where G is "threaded."

When introducing these notes, octave designations (such as "low" F or "middle" G) are not necessary and can be confusing.

Once the child understands the relationship between the line, the sound, and the keyboard position, they should not only read and play the newly learned notes but should also write them in the regular homework notebook using a black pen or pencil. It's best for the child to reproduce both #41 and #42 and compare their written work to the models in Volume One. They will see the familiar colored notes and compare them to the sounds they have written in traditional black notation.

Many children like to write their own songs and to draw their own notes on paper. Sometimes they will use the musical staff; other times they will draw only colored note heads without staff lines. Although they may not always place the colored notes in their correct places on the musical staff, the teacher should let the child play these pieces corresponding to the colors, offering encouragement and support.

The note area can be expanded using the same methods. For the bass clef, it's best to expand upward from F to B; for treble, downward from G to D. This must be reinforced with meaningful homework. As more notes are introduced, the homework becomes more demanding. The written notes should always be compared with corresponding pieces from *We Hear and Play*— not only to check accuracy, but also to make the connection between the colored and non-colored notes.

Once all the notes are introduced, the student may be shown the accidental symbols: sharp, flat, and natural. To do this, the teacher says the names of each symbol out loud and lets the child find the symbols in the *We Hear and Play* book. The symbols appear in the following pieces:

(sharp): Volume Two, #148; Volume Three, #212, 218, 228, 229, 231

♭ (flat): Volume One, #64, 89, 91, 93, 97; Volume Two, #137, 145, 188; Volume Three, #210, 217, 261, 265, 266

♮ (natural): Volume Three, #280

The child's homework is to write a full line of each symbol, as they did the clefs. After practicing this a while, they can write down any of the *We Hear and Play* pieces which feature the accidental symbols, which will include F-sharp, B-flat, and F-natural. The adult should check the homework to make sure the symbols' staff positions are accurate. The child may now be explicitly told that an accidental symbol applies to an entire measure.

Next the teacher may point out middle C's ledger line in each clef, using #27 and #28. The child should be guided to practice writing middle C with the same spacing as the other lines on the staff. This is why writing middle C is more difficult than reading it.

To supplement reading and writing practice, absolute listening must be gradually expanded into active absolute pitch (see "Definition of Absolute Pitch," page 76). While reviewing the written homework, the teacher prompts the child to sing each pitch that has been written, without the help of a piano or other pitch reference. This type of practice should be used for all pitch sounds. **Without this training, the child's absolute pitch ability may remain permanently passive.** The child should learn low C to middle C on the bass staff and middle C to high C on the treble staff. These pitches should be practiced until reading, writing, hearing, singing, and playing become open and free.

The next step is to write the notes of an entire piece, including clef symbols and measure lines. We recommend using short pieces for this new step, such as #127, #128, #131, and #132 in Volume Two, and later, #274, #275, #282, and #283 from Volume Three, which include the time signature. The Stomper signs should be omitted from all these pieces.

This is how a child can learn fundamental musical ideas: different notes and rests, measure lines, and time signatures. Practicing with suitable pieces from all three volumes of *We Hear and Play*, the child also becomes acquainted with the use of the grand staff for two-handed piano playing.

Once a new task is introduced, it should be repeated until the child has *complete* control of it. As a basic principle, especially in this stage, the child's strengths should be praised and their weaknesses avoided.

When the child is introduced to traditional notation, the piano's white keys are still marked with colored dots. The colored dots, like the colored notes, shouldn't be removed too early. The child uses the dots for orientation to find the keys they want to play. Colored dots and colored notes are needed throughout all three volumes of *We Hear and Play* as well as during the child's introduction to easy piano literature. It's a bad idea to try to teach traditional notation by removing the colored dots and notes, thus depriving the child of two important aids to orientation and comprehension.

Removing the colored dots should begin with yellow, orange, grey, and purple. The red, green, and blue dots should remain for quick reference. When the child succeeds with only these dots, the green dots can then be removed so that only red and blue are available.

The length of time these final two dots remain on the keyboard differs for each child and, naturally, depends on the difficulty level of the pieces they play. In any case, it is much better to use colored dots and make progress than to remove the dots and stagnate.

Beyond We Hear and Play

This chapter explains how *We Hear and Play* training can be continued, when the child has completed the three volumes this handbook covers (see also "Timeline of a Child's Musical Development," page 83). A child will normally finish Volume Three before developing complete absolute pitch. The process is different for each individual, absolute pitch deveopment does not always proceed at the same pace as acquiring piano skills. At the conclusion of Volume Three, one child may recognize all the white keys within an octave; another child may hear all the white keys and some black keys (like F-sharp and B-flat) and occasionally all 12 pitch sounds.

Absolute pitch training is an essential component of all further piano training. The three chords (I, II, and III) are still the base for developing hearing skills, but new, carefully planned hearing exercises and games should be added to promote further progress. The planning should not merely cover each new lesson as it occurs but should consider long-term goals.

The curriculum should be tailored for each child. The teacher must be flexible, presenting the material according to the child's progress and modifying it as necessary. It isn't necessary to do *all* these exercises— for hearing development, rhythmic training, piano technique, and reading traditional notation— at each and every lesson. Sometimes it can be useful to spend an entire lesson on a single exercise; or, if it becomes meaningful to reinforce an exercise with additional games, this could be a lesson's principal component.

When one exercise dominates a lesson, this allows little time for other tasks. An extension of the lesson is usually not helpful, even if the participants' schedules allow it, because the child's ability to concentrate will become exhausted from this focused effort.

Focused studies should be done separately from regular lessons, because the child will have practiced homework from the previous lesson. If what the child has practiced is not dealt with in the lesson, the child may be disappointed, which can disturb their daily practice routine. Therefore, it's important to announce any special lesson ahead of time, so that the child prepares all their work for the regular lesson after that.

One might suppose that intensive instruction would cause accelerated development in those areas. However, any significant changes in the child's development will only become evident after many months of training.

For further development of piano playing skill, we must clarify which pieces the child should play, which we do in the next section. We repeat: it is *absolutely necessary* to allow the child to continue to play with colored notes. The traditional notation should be introduced only after certain prerequisites have been met (described in "Introducing Traditional Notation," page 59).

Playing New Music

Selecting Musical Pieces

We have pre-selected no general repertoire of pieces, because the child's personality should be considered in each new choice. However, we can specify some criteria to help guide these choices.

All pieces should appeal to the child musically. Children are very different in their preferences: some prefer simple but lively pieces, while others prefer songs with rich harmonic changes. Sometimes a child wants to play the same pieces over and over; sometimes a child wants new pieces.

The teacher should make sure the child is not required to make great leaps in playing technique. That is, new techniques should be introduced gradually. This applies to new fingerings, thumb support, arpeggios, and different chords as well as to new key signatures.

Most pieces should be in C-major, although G-major, D-major, and a-minor can be used. F-major and B-major are hard for children. Although some of the more difficult key sounds do appear in *We Hear and Play*, caution and patience should be used with songs in these key signatures. Our key signature guidelines are

- Most pieces should be in C-major.

- A piece in G-major should be followed by additional pieces in G-major.

- After playing G-major songs, several C-major pieces should be chosen in succession.

- Later, pieces may alternate between G-major and C-major.

- Subsequent pieces can be in A-minor, D-major, or F-major.

Overall, C-major should form the kernel of the pieces a child plays over any period of several months. Each key signature except C is unfamiliar territory, so the child needs time to become acquainted with it. The child should become familiar with each key sound in turn so that they can eventually change between them without difficulty. If the teacher develops a good feeling for introducing new key signatures, they can more easily judge the appropriateness of the literature while also accommodating concerns about fingering complexity and playing technique. A teacher should be able to choose pieces for the child which are not too hard, but slightly challenging, and above all interesting.

The question remains: when and how should the child be introduced to modern music? *We Hear and Play* includes some relatively modern pieces and some of Béla Bartók's work. The majority of the pieces, however, are in the major-minor system. Understandably, most pieces are in major keys. Part of the goal of

We Hear and Play is to develop a feeling for classic harmony and a subconscious recognition of harmonic structure.

If this goal is pursued by adept and consistent musical selection and improvisation, then the child can better understand the variations of modern musical structure. They will better recognize its departure from major-minor harmony as well as its other stylistic nuances. Each modern piece should be introduced with a clear objective in mind, which means that the proportion of modern to classical pieces will be small.

We can recommend suitable collections which meet the needs of older children with meaningfully selected and organized pieces. Our specific recommendations, each of which has meaningfully selected and organized pieces printed with child-friendly large notes, on our website (www.wehearandplay.com).

In addition to the selection of pieces, the quantity of pieces must be decided for each child. For a child who is progressing normally, the selected pieces should never be too hard, and the child should not be given too many pieces to play at once. Nevertheless, the pieces should promote pedagogical measures to improve the child's skill.

A child who can learn songs quickly and play them with fluidity and skill should learn several pieces simultaneously. This means the teacher must find many suitable pieces of similar difficulty, which isn't easy to do. The teacher is often tempted to jump up to a higher difficulty level, and let the child play an excessively difficult piece. Such a jump is pedagogically meaningless, and is more likely to damage the child's enjoyment of playing.

Coloring the Notes

During the transition from colored to traditional notes, it is imperative to paint colors over the black note heads. This is as important as having colored dots on the piano keys. A colored pencil is best; a felt-tip pen soaks through the paper and shows on the other side. Moreover, felt-tip color cannot be removed, while colored pencils can be erased. The best way to color the notes is to draw a line around the note, so that the child clearly recognizes the colored note edge; this way, half notes can be colored without filling in the hole in the middle of the note.

As was described in the chapter "Introducing Traditional Notation," the teacher and parents shouldn't move away from the colors too quickly. It is wrong to give the child the impression that the colored notes are abnormal or somehow worse than the black-and-white system. The child would then feel pressured to stop using the colored notes. On the other hand, if the people in the child's environment (parents, siblings, friends) respond positively to the colored notes, the child will be willing to keep using them. In any case, colored notes and traditionally printed notes should be used together over several years for a child's well-balanced education.

First, the teacher paints color onto the black notes. By now the parents are usually familiar with the *We Hear and Play* colors and can color the notes themselves, but if they have trouble reading the notes, the teacher must help. Siblings and friends can often help as well.

Printed Notes

Printed notes for children should be large. The younger the child, the more important this is. This fact was given special consideration in the three volumes of *We Hear and Play*. This need is becoming more widely recognized and more music with large print is being produced. If large-print notes are not available, one can try to switch between large and small notes, but a child should never be forced to read small notes.

Obviously, more sizes exist than simply "large" and "small." The quality of the printing or the paper itself can play an important role in good legibility. All these factors should be taken into account when choosing instructional material.

Many times a teacher believes a certain note size will suffice for a child, only to notice later that the child is unhappy with the music. The child's attitude may be improved by transferring the music to larger notes. In this situation, it is also often helpful for a child at an advanced level to repeat the three volumes of *We Hear and Play*, either partially or entirely.

Developing Advanced Piano Technique

Two-handed Coordination

Different children have wildly different abilities to coordinate both hands. Children normally learn to play songs first with each hand separately; then they play together (with some effort). Some 4-year-old children show no coordination problems at all, and can immediately play a new piece with both hands together. These children's practices can be more complicated. In other cases, children are able to play with one hand but find it hard to use both. This bias can persist until age 7 or 8, and even age 12 in extreme cases.

Practicing Piano Technique

In advanced stages of instruction, with older students, it is important to practice piano technique. Whether a piece should be chosen for the purpose of teaching a particular technique is debatable, but technical practice always has at least an indirect connection with the music being played; and pieces can be found which improve the general quality of the child's piano playing.

In the *We Hear and Play* selections there are obvious distinctions between practices and musical pieces, but a child won't tell the difference. The child finds

practices such as #119 and #223 just as interesting as actual songs. With
continuing instruction, after finishing the three volumes of *We Hear and Play*,
non-songs can be chosen as practice pieces. The teacher should develop their own
ideas and invent practices from case to case. The essential matter is, above all,
that pieces should be selected for their technical contribution to the student's
education. If the teacher succeeds in sustaining the child's interest in the
technical practices— and playing the pieces is a firm component of each lesson—
the child will continue to practice at home as well.

Older children may resist playing technical practices every day. They
sometimes perceive these as a burden.

For initial practice in playing technique, a three-note combination is best
(from #33 and #34 in Volume One):

A four-note combination may follow:

As is shown in Volume Three, #270-273, the teacher can accompany this
practice in higher or lower octaves (or on a second piano). As an accompaniment,
it is good to choose a phrase of 4 to 8 measures. It should fit with the note
combinations the child is repeating and also be a pleasant piece of music. The
accompaniment can be repeated or played in variations along with the child.

With the teacher's accompaniment, the playing proceeds toward
improvisation. A teacher who does not yet have much experience with
improvisation may compose in advance a 4- to 8-measure song to accompany the
child. A teacher who is experienced in improvisation must be careful not to
improvise music that is too complicated; although a child may by this time have
developed absolute pitch from *We Hear and Play*, they are still not capable of
following complex harmonic, melodic, and rhythmic structures. If the
accompaniment becomes too complicated, the child may find themselves unable
to follow along with it, which leads to the undesirable habit of not listening to the
accompaniment at all, a habit often observed in children practicing music.

Examples of useful practices and note combinations can be found in Hans
Kann's book (see literature recommendations, page 98). Although the practices
suitable for this age group are intended to be played within the two middle
octaves, they can be expanded over the entire keyboard. Instead of sitting in front
of the keyboard, the child may want to stand up and move to reach both ends of
the instrument. This exploration may allow the child to play familiar pieces in
higher or lower octaves; and doing this in practice contributes to the expansion of
the child's absolute pitch into higher and lower pitch sounds.

As we have previously explained, absolute pitch does not necessarily develop in all octaves simultaneously. If a child hears middle G absolutely, they will not necessarily be able to identify high G. Additional training is usually required. The practice of moving around the entire keyboard helps the child hear the sounds of all the white keys, although this is not the only exercise necessary for expanding the absolute ear (see page 58).

The child also discovers that, in different areas of the piano keyboard, a different attack is needed to produce a good sound. Through this discovery the child develops a good feeling for how they will play in these areas.

Finally, returning to the subject of practicing technique: even if, for whatever reason, a child abandons the habit of practicing at home and therefore only practices with the teacher at their lesson, this is still better than eliminating technical practices altogether. The child will continue to improve their technique with each weekly lesson, due to the high speed of childhood physical and mental development.

Four-handed Playing

"Four-handed" playing, in which the teacher and child play together, is very helpful. In selecting suitable pieces, the teacher should use the same criteria as for solo pieces, that is, of musical content and note size. Technical leaps in fingering and placement should be avoided. Any grown-up can participate and be a playing partner. Usually this is the child's teacher, of course, but at home it can be a parent or older sibling. If no partner is available at home, and they have a good relationship with the teacher, the child can play their part alone and will look forward to playing with the teacher in the next lesson.

The teacher will discover that many children are enthusiastic about playing "four-handed," but others are reluctant. We have seen extreme examples of children refusing to play with their teacher. When confronted with a child who refuses to play with them, the teacher may try to distract the child with a story. While the child plays their part, but with their attention divided, the teacher may play softly. If the child thus experiences the delight of the four-handed game and lets down their inner barriers, this will make the game a success for both the child and the teacher.

If the teacher's attempts remain unsuccessful, and the child stubbornly refuses to play with them, the cause is most likely psychological. In such cases the solution is beyond the teacher's responsibility, and a conversation with the parents becomes necessary.

What should the ratio be between solo pieces and four-handed playing? The child should play more solo than four-handed within any given period. Sometimes, if the child finds it especially entertaining and the teacher finds it especially meaningful, the entire lesson can be devoted to four-handed playing; however, in the next lesson the teacher should return to the normal ratio.

Four-handed playing is beneficial to the child's musical growth for several reasons. One is that the child cannot interrupt a piece. This unspoken obligation is helpful, since children often show a strong inclination to stop in the middle of their playing. Also, certain unrhythmic biases can be corrected when the teacher plays along in accurate rhythm. Further, it leads to an improvement of harmonic sense, because the harmony cannot be changed at will. At the same time the child discovers that variations are possible within the same harmony.

The main disadvantage of the four handed game is that a child cannot always monitor their own sound quality and playing technique. A further disadvantage can be that a child does not take personal initiative in this activity. This can have negative consequences for children who tend to be passive.

Although a long list of advantages and disadvantages could be compiled, it's most helpful to recommend that the teacher observe the child carefully and develop solo and team practices appropriate to the child's strengths and weaknesses.

Advanced Skills

Transposing

Transposition has special importance in ongoing piano instruction. Absolute pitch is a prerequisite for transposition. Each child has had some exposure to transposition already, in *We Hear and Play* Volume Three, #211 and #212, in which the same song is played in two different key signatures.

The child should be encouraged to transpose a piece which they have played for a long time and know extremely well. It should be in C-major and have classical harmonic structure. The child should not begin by transposing into a similar key, such as G-major or F-major. Instead, the song should initially be transposed one whole tone higher (D-major). At first most children will play in D-minor; then the teacher may recommend using the black key (F-sharp). After this experience, the children may find for themselves other keys in which the piece can be played.

It is not wise to transpose a piece into too many keys. It is better to concentrate on only one or two, solidifying the transposition process with new pieces in those few keys, rather than distracting from the process with the multiple variant sounds.

Improvising and Developing Harmonic Feeling

The four-handed game, technical practice, and improvisation are all closely related. The last of these, improvisation, should now be explored, because improvisation practices are especially meaningful to children with absolute pitch. After a successful introduction to improvisation, these children will soon discover the creative side of piano playing, and their musical experience will be tremendously enriched.

Improvising should only be attempted at a degree of difficulty comfortable for the child, in a way that's appropriate to the child's understanding of music and playing technique. Almost all children will remain at a specific stage of improvisation for quite a long while.

Improvising is best if the child and the teacher play together on two pianos. If this is impossible, the two may use the same piano, but they don't need to play with all four hands. They can play with two hands (child and teacher each playing one-handed) or three hands (child playing two-handed and teacher one-handed, or vice versa).

The best way to start is for the teacher to present a simple combination from two different pitches (and later three) which the child can consider before playing. The resemblance between this exercise and the now-familiar technical practice helps. After the teacher has played the simple combination, the child should repeat it and, through repetition, establish a rhythm. The teacher then supplements and develops the child's melody fragment. A child at the beginning level continues to play mainly by following the teacher while a more advanced student begins to create a kind of dialogue. At the same time the teacher can carefully support the emerging melody with a bass line or with harmonies.

In parallel with melodic improvisation the child can be guided to harmonic improvisation. They have already come in contact with simple harmonies via the sounds of chords I, II, and III, and these sounds become the foundation for harmonic playing. It is on this basis that the child, with the support of the absolute pitch sense they have developed, can be introduced to harmonic structure.

As an initial goal, it is desirable for the child to understand the emotional character of the three main chords within C-major and use them accordingly. The child can improvise harmoniously with the teacher from this foundation. Improvisation also involves inventing a chord sequence, keeping to a time signature, dividing each measure properly, and keeping tempo. Adults who are not familiar with principles of improvisation find it complicated; but for a child who has fulfilled the prerequisites mentioned above, it becomes simple, especially if they have played with the same model several times.

Another way to approach improvisation is to take a few measures from a piano piece that the child has just played— perhaps only a small part of its theme— and use that as a subject for improvisation. This can be done not only with the melody, but also with interesting harmonic or rhythmic sequences.

At more advanced levels, a child who has developed absolute pitch from *We Hear and Play* can "play by ear," simultaneously grasping melody, harmony, and rhythm when imitating a well-known musical piece. Such imitations can later lead them to their own attempts at composing.

Many music teachers discover that their own education has not prepared them for improvisation, and they find themselves questioning their own ability. Not many publications teach piano improvisation, but there is one which can be informative and useful: *Improvisation at the Piano*, by Haim Alexander (two volumes with cassettes), Schott ED7536

Overtaxing a Child

Occasionally, one child proves more adept, intelligent, and capable than others. This creates the danger that the teacher will give them unusually difficult pieces. But being forced into an abnormally high level of performance does not help the child's development. Furthermore, it can become an emotional burden for the child— the stress of taking on complicated pieces destroying the joy of piano playing.

Piano competitions are a tempting target for the enthusiastic parent or teacher, but competitions don't add much to a child's training. The parent's competitive desires can be satisfied by other means: perhaps private recitals can be arranged with students of similar ability, using pieces suitable to their level. However, frequent recitals have little influence on improving a child's musical development.

Although the children raised with *We Hear and Play* training should spend a respectable amount of time on daily practice, this must be balanced with normal activity in order for the child to have a positive outlook on life. A balanced, well-adjusted personality is, in our view, the main goal of any child's upbringing.

Appendices

Definition of Absolute Pitch

Absolute pitch can be generally described as "the ability to recognize pitches without relative references." However, there are different levels of this ability.

1. *Absolute hearing of a specific pitch*

   Many musicians can hear one certain pitch absolutely. This sound is usually a middle C, although it is sometimes middle D or A.

2. *Absolute hearing of multiple pitches*

   This is an expansion of level 1, although the pitches differ from person to person. Sometimes only C is recognized, but in many different octaves. Other people may recognize only middle C and G, or perhaps C, D, G, and A.

3. *Absolute hearing of C-major pitches in narrow range*

   Many people can recognize a small range of C-major piano sounds (the white keys). They may, for example, recognize all the white notes between G and C, predominantly in the middle octave. The upper and lower ranges vary from person to person at this level.

4. *Absolute hearing of all C-major pitches*

   At this level all C-major piano sounds can be recognized— all the white keys, but not necessarily the black keys.

5. *Absolute hearing of all pitches in limited range*

   At this level all pitches in a certain area can be identified; for example, between low C and high C. The boundary between the pitches which are and are not absolutely recognized is not always distinct.

6. *Condition-contingent absolute hearing*

   In this variant of absolute hearing, listeners from any of the previous levels can apply their ability only when in a good physical and mental state. Consequently, there are people who, in unfavorable conditions, can recognize only one or two absolute sounds, but in good conditions can recognize a larger number.

7. *Timbre-contingent absolute hearing*

Sometimes, pitches can only be recognized on one type of instrument—and sometimes only on one specific instrument. Any of the previous levels can appear in different combinations: for example, a person may be able to *identify* only the sounds of a certain piano in unfavorable conditions, while under good conditions that same person can recognize sounds from any piano or other instrument.

8. *Absolute hearing connected with musical production*

Many people can internalize a musical piece and hear it especially well in memory. Its beginning, or a precise section of it, can strongly impress a pitch or key-*signature* sensation upon them. This ability is typically also condition-contingent. Additionally, many people can identify pitches based on the boundary of their singing voice, or by focusing their voice on a specific pitch. The examples in this category, however, all concern a relative sequence of sounds based on an imaginary reference sound. This category does not truly belong to our definition of absolute pitch.

9. *Complete absolute hearing*

This level supercedes all previous ones. It is the ability to hear, irrespective of conditions, all musical sounds of any instrument as well as the human *voice*. Compared to this level, the others can described as "incomplete" absolute pitch.

10. *Active complete absolute hearing*

People with complete absolute hearing can imagine pitch sounds in their mind, and they can recreate those sounds by singing them. We call this "active absolute pitch." *We Hear and Play* strives for this level of absolute hearing as its principal goal.

Most people with this active ability also recognize pitches from any source. Sometimes, however, a person may have this active ability but also have incomplete absolute pitch. Children who are developing absolute pitch by means of *We Hear and Play* will pass through several of the levels before they achieve complete active absolute pitch.

Frequently Asked Questions About Absolute Pitch

1. *How can a teacher assess a student's absolute pitch ability, if the student has already been studying music?*

   An experienced teacher may intuitively recognize a student's ability during their first lesson. Alternately, the teacher can prompt the student to play a piece from memory, but starting in the middle of the song. A student with absolute pitch can do this easily. However, the simplest method is to let the students hear and name single tones, or reproduce sounds on a second instrument following this procedure:

   The teacher plays a sound on one instrument. The student names this sound or plays it on a second instrument. If named correctly, this tone becomes a reference, so the teacher's next choice should not be adjacent to it, nor form a fourth, fifth, or octave with it. If the student correctly names or reproduces the new sound, the teacher continues the test in the same manner. If the student always answers correctly, it means that they definitely have absolute pitch.

2. *How can a teacher assess a student who has incomplete absolute hearing? What if the student hears partially (levels 1-4) or conditionally (levels 6-7)?*

   This test is somewhat more difficult. The teacher can't simply ask outright because the student is rarely aware of their ability. Because absolute hearing often occurs with middle C, the teacher might first check the student's ability to recognize this pitch and then test other pitches at other times. In some cases it takes many class sessions before it becomes clear that the student has absolute pitch for a limited number of tones. In the best-case scenario this testing will activate the student's previously concealed absolute pitch ability.

3. *Why should we assess a student's absolute hearing ability?*

   It's important for planning the student's training. The teacher should plan further development of the student's hearing ability via ear training, and a student with absolute hearing is more immersed in their music and can command a larger repertoire than a student who doesn't hear absolutely. If the student is unable to hear absolutely, the teacher must approach each new assignment more carefully. Also, the student's hearing ability should be improved; if the student can already hear some tones absolutely, the teacher can work to expand this ability.

4. *If someone hears one pitch absolutely, and has strong "relative pitch", isn't this equivalent to absolute pitch?*

   The relative ear develops gradually, in connection with theoretical understanding of the entire musical system. A student's theoretical understanding is directly connected to their intelligence, interest in music, and accumulated musical experiences (such as attending concerts or playing in ensembles). It is unlikely that a young child would have advanced relative ability. Absolute pitch is a tremendous musical advantage for children. As they develop into their musicianship, strong relative skills become necessary, regardless of their absolute hearing ability.

5. *But how does relative pitch affect an older student, or an adult? Does good relative pitch replace absolute pitch?*

   Well-developed relative pitch often provides a more sophisticated understanding than absolute pitch, especially if the absolute ear is not sufficiently trained or meaningfully used. But even when someone achieves a high degree of relative pitch, and is able to reproduce an entire scale from a single reference sound, there are still advantages to be gained from absolute perception.

6. *How does absolute pitch ability develop in a person who has had no systematic training from which to learn it?*

   Most often, this happens when people come into contact with an instrument at an early age. For instance, they begin early with piano or violin instruction, and while training, a type of unconscious didactic listening takes place. This listening is especially attentive to pitches and is not affected by unfavorable environmental factors. (For a list of negative conditions and factors, see page 59).

   In some cases listeners are trained to hear absolutely— not systematically, but at least deliberately and consistently— and this approach has been successful in a proportion of students.

7. *Won't someone with absolute pitch always know they have it?*

   Although most people do know, some people are not aware of their ability.

8. *Can adults with absolute pitch remember how and when their ability emerged?*

   Someone who has received systematic ear-training instruction, such as *We Hear and Play*, can usually explain how their absolute pitch developed. There are, however, examples of children learning inadvertently:

1. A man whose father was a professional violinist remembers how his father played the empty strings when tuning his violin. The pitches of the empty strings were impressed on him, especially the middle D, and became the basis of his absolute pitch ability. He later became a composer.

2. Another performer attended church regularly with his father, who was the organist. The organ sounds became the basis for his absolute ear. He later became a pianist who commanded an unusually extensive repertoire of modern music from memory. This would be unimaginable without absolute pitch.

Many people cannot explain how their ability developed. In most of these cases the origin of their absolute ear occurred in earliest childhood. The events of that time are isolated, disconnected memories which can no longer be reconstructed.

9. *Why would a person fail to gain absolute pitch if, in early childhood, they were in contact with an instrument or had instrumental instruction?*

There were probably too many negative factors in the environment. (For negative factors in absolute pitch education, see page 59.) They also may have had little interest in pitch sounds.

10. *Do adults sometimes discover that they have absolute pitch, even though they were not exposed to music as a child?*

This does happen. Their ability is often discovered by other people—usually music teachers. As mentioned, these adults can't remember their early childhood years, but their absolute pitch development may have resulted from musical impressions they received from their environment: perhaps from television or radio, church bells, or other pitch sounds they listened to attentively.

11. *What advantages does someone actually gain from absolute pitch?*

A person with absolute pitch is better at playing music. But this simple answer does not say much. Let us elaborate:

1. Children with absolute pitch can quickly memorize and reproduce musical pieces on their instruments.

2. During musical instruction these children can react immediately to the teacher's voice. If the teacher sings a note, instead of naming it, the child finds the corresponding key and plays it. The child's hand goes to the correct key almost unconsciously.

3. Musicians with absolute hearing can easily read and imagine musical notes, and they are better at retaining musical pieces in memory. With absolute pitch, a musician can control a larger repertoire since they can memorize many pieces simultaneously.

4. A performer with absolute pitch has a higher sense of security even when conditions are stressful due to excitement or nervousness. They can therefore play before the public more confidently and without problems.

5. Practicing and memorizing a piece requires relatively little time. This is especially beneficial for adult amateurs who pursue other occupations and have little time for practicing.

6. A person with absolute hearing can better follow a musical performance. They can recognize the structure of the musical pieces more quickly and thoroughly, particularly with contemporary or modern music. This allows them to more firmly grasp its contents, more fully enriching their intellectual life.

7. Absolute listeners have a great advantage in an ensemble. They can listen well to other instruments and still retain an overview of the music.

8. Largely for this reason, absolute hearing has great advantages for directing, especially modern music.

12. *Is absolute hearing a disadvantage in transposing, because a piece can only be "heard" in the original key?*

Absolute pitch is an advantage in transposing, but the absolute listener must be well trained. With the help of their relative ear, a musician with absolute pitch can intellectually transpose a musical piece into another key. Then they can reproduce this new key more easily on their instrument.

13. *Do absolute listeners have difficulty in playing instruments that are tuned differently?*

The absolute listener will initially be confused. After some time for habituation, however, they can adjust their thinking to the new pitches. This is similar to transposing, in that the absolute listener mentally forms a new sound scale. After this scale is formed, the absolute musician can play it more easily.

14. *What if a singer in a choir must sing a work that has been transposed to another key?*

    This is essentially the same situation: a person with a well-trained absolute ear can "turn off" the absolute characteristic of the song in some respects. They can then sing confidently in the new key with the benefit of their absolute pitch.

15. *Can someone who learned absolute pitch at certain specific frequencies manage to play a differently-tuned instrument?*

    If their absolute ear is trained well, the person will have no trouble. During the education phase, the instruments used at home and for instruction must be exactly and equally tuned. The tuning must be controlled to ensure that the pitch sounds are constant. After their absolute ear has stabilized, the student can adjust to different tunings. A well-trained absolute ear is elastic and adaptable, and can identify pitches even from an out-of-tune piano.

16. *Can someone with absolute pitch estimate their own ability?*

    Many people think that the term "absolute pitch" only applies to active absolute pitch (level 10). Therefore, someone with incomplete absolute pitch may think they don't have any absolute hearing ability.

17. *Once learned, is absolute pitch permanent, or can it be lost?*

    If an infant is trained in absolute pitch, the ability can be lost if the regular listening exercises are neglected. (See "Absolute Pitch Training", page 8.)

    There are adults who say they possessed absolute pitch as a child but lost it during adulthood. In these cases they often mean that they had active absolute pitch at one time, but now can only demonstrate passive absolute pitch. It is conceivable that their absolute pitch instruction was inadequate; it is also possible that increasing age makes it harder for them to imagine accurate pitch sounds.